"Unveiling Pain: The Global Impact of COVID-19"

Swatantra Bahadur

Published by Swatantra Bahadur, 2024.

While every precaution has been taken in the preparation of this book, the publisher assumes no responsibility for errors or omissions, or for damages resulting from the use of the information contained herein.

"UNVEILING PAIN: THE GLOBAL IMPACT OF COVID-19"

First edition. January 25, 2024.

Copyright © 2024 Swatantra Bahadur.

ISBN: 979-8224853892

Written by Swatantra Bahadur.

Disclaimer

The information presented in this book is intended for general informational purposes only and should not be relied upon as a substitute for professional advice or judgment. The author and publisher are not responsible for any action taken by readers based on the information provided in this book. Readers should seek appropriate professional advice or conduct their own research before making decisions related to the topics discussed in this book. The views expressed in this book are those of the author and do not necessarily reflect the views of the publisher.

Content

Introduction

In the wake of the unprecedented COVID-19 pandemic, the world found itself ensnared in an intricate web of pain—physical, emotional, economic, and social. "Unveiling Pain: The Global Impact of COVID-19" is an exploration into the multifaceted layers of suffering that swept across continents, leaving no corner of the globe untouched. This book endeavors to unravel the intricate tapestry of challenges, resilience, and transformations that have defined the human experience during these tumultuous times.

The chapters within these pages delve into the profound human toll exacted by the virus, examining the staggering loss of lives, the enduring health repercussions, and the relentless strain on healthcare systems. As we traverse through the economic fallout, we witness the far-reaching consequences of a global recession, with businesses shuttering, employment plummeting, and economic disparities widening. The educational landscape, too, undergoes a seismic shift, with schools and universities grappling with closures and the digital divide laying bare the inequalities in access to education.

The narrative extends beyond statistics and charts, weaving through the intricacies of mental health struggles—how isolation and grief have left an indelible mark on the collective psyche. Amidst the chaos, the strain on healthcare systems becomes a poignant chapter, with frontline workers battling exhaustion and resource shortages, and the challenge of equitable vaccine distribution underscoring the global community's interconnectedness.

Social and cultural norms, once steadfast, bend and reshape under the weight of the pandemic. The spread of misinformation and fear adds another layer of complexity to the social fabric, challenging the foundations of trust and cooperation. Yet, within these narratives of pain, we uncover stories of hope, resilience, and the innate human capacity to rise above adversity. Communities come together, innovation flourishes, and lessons are learned that can shape a more resilient future.

"Unveiling Pain" seeks to capture the collective human experience during this pivotal moment in history. It is a call to understand, empathize, and reflect on the interconnectedness of our global society. As we navigate through the shadows of pain, the book aims to illuminate the path towards healing, unity, and the promise of a brighter post-pandemic future.

A. Brief overview of the COVID-19 pandemic

The COVID-19 pandemic, caused by the novel coronavirus SARS-CoV-2, stands as one of the most impactful global crises in recent history. Emerging in late 2019 in the city of Wuhan, Hubei province, China, the virus swiftly traversed international borders, triggering a worldwide health emergency. Characterized by its high transmission rate, the virus led to a respiratory illness known as COVID-19.

Governments and healthcare systems worldwide faced an unprecedented challenge in containing the virus's spread and mitigating its impact. The World Health Organization (WHO) declared the outbreak a pandemic on March 11, 2020, acknowledging its widespread prevalence and the urgency of coordinated global response efforts.

The pandemic disrupted daily life on an extraordinary scale, prompting widespread lockdowns, travel restrictions, and social distancing measures. These measures, while critical for public health, had profound repercussions on economies, education, and societal norms. The virus, with its ability to cause severe respiratory distress and its propensity for asymptomatic spread, placed immense strain on healthcare infrastructures globally.

Efforts to curb the pandemic included widespread testing, contact tracing, and the rapid development and deployment of vaccines. The pandemic's progression varied across regions, influenced by factors such as public health measures, healthcare capabilities, and vaccine distribution.

Beyond its immediate health implications, the pandemic revealed and exacerbated existing societal inequalities, economic disparities, and vulnerabilities in global healthcare systems. As nations grappled with the human toll, economic downturns, and the complexities of vaccination campaigns, the COVID-19 pandemic became a defining moment that underscored the interconnectedness of our world and the need for collaborative, innovative solutions to address global challenges.

B. Importance of understanding the global impact of the pandemic

Understanding the global impact of the COVID-19 pandemic is paramount for several reasons, as it transcends the realms of public health and touches upon various facets of human existence. Delving into this global phenomenon is crucial for the following reasons:

Humanitarian Perspective

a. Loss of Lives: The pandemic has resulted in a staggering loss of lives worldwide. Understanding the full scope of this tragedy fosters empathy and solidarity with those who have suffered, acknowledging the collective grief shared globally.

b. Health Inequities: Examining the disparities in healthcare outcomes across different regions sheds light on existing health inequities. This knowledge is instrumental in advocating for more inclusive and accessible healthcare systems.

Economic Implications

a. Global Recession: The pandemic triggered a widespread economic downturn, affecting industries, businesses, and individuals. Analyzing the economic fallout helps in devising strategies for recovery, addressing unemployment, and building more resilient economies.

b. Supply Chain Disruptions: The disruption of global supply chains highlighted vulnerabilities in interconnected economies. Studying these disruptions informs strategies to enhance resilience and adaptability in the face of future crises.

Educational and Social Consequences

a. Educational Disruption: The closure of schools and universities disrupted education globally. Understanding the challenges faced by students, educators, and institutions is crucial for shaping future educational strategies and ensuring equitable access to learning.

b. Social Dynamics: The pandemic has reshaped social norms, affecting how people interact, work, and communicate. Examining these changes provides insights into societal resilience, adaptation, and the evolution of cultural practices.

Public Health Preparedness

a. Lesson Learning: Analyzing the global response to the pandemic helps identify both successes and shortcomings in public health strategies. This knowledge is invaluable for refining future preparedness and response efforts.

b. Vaccine Distribution: Understanding the challenges and successes in vaccine distribution on a global scale informs ongoing efforts to achieve widespread vaccination coverage and address health disparities.

International Collaboration

a. Interconnectedness: The pandemic highlighted the interconnected nature of the global community. Recognizing the importance of international collaboration in responding to crises fosters a sense of shared responsibility and encourages cooperative efforts in addressing other global challenges.

Crisis Management and Resilience

a. Resilience Building: Analyzing how different nations coped with the pandemic enhances our understanding of effective crisis management and resilience-building strategies. These insights can guide future preparedness for pandemics and other global crises.

In essence, comprehending the global impact of the COVID-19 pandemic is not just about understanding the past; it is about gaining the knowledge and insights necessary to shape a more resilient, equitable, and interconnected future for humanity.

C. Purpose of the book: to explore the multifaceted pain experienced worldwide

The purpose of "Unveiling Pain: The Global Impact of COVID-19" is to embark on a comprehensive exploration of the multifaceted pain that has reverberated across the globe during the unprecedented COVID-19 pandemic. This book seeks to delve into the intricate layers of suffering, resilience, and transformation that have defined the human experience in the face of this formidable crisis.

Holistic Understanding

a. Human Toll: The book aims to provide a nuanced understanding of the profound human toll exacted by the virus, exploring the experiences of individuals, families, and communities who have grappled with illness, loss, and the enduring health effects of COVID-19.

b. Economic Fallout: Delving into the economic repercussions, the book examines the pain caused by widespread unemployment, business closures, and the exacerbation of existing inequalities, offering a comprehensive view of the economic struggles faced globally.

c. Educational Disruption: By exploring the educational disruptions, the book sheds light on the challenges faced by students, educators, and educational institutions, recognizing the pain caused by the interruption of learning and the digital divide.

Emphasis on Mental Health

a. Isolation and Grief: The book places a significant focus on the mental health struggles induced by isolation, grief, and the collective trauma experienced by societies worldwide, aiming to destigmatize and raise awareness about the importance of mental well-being.

b. Healthcare Strain: Understanding the strain on healthcare systems and frontline workers is crucial to appreciating the emotional toll on those battling the pandemic on the front lines. The book explores the challenges faced by healthcare professionals and the impact on their mental and emotional well-being.

Social and Cultural Dynamics

a. Shifts in Norms: Through an examination of social and cultural disruptions, the book elucidates how societal norms and behaviors have shifted, exploring the pain caused by the alteration of daily life and the reshaping of social interactions.

b. Rise in Misinformation: Addressing the rise in misinformation and fear, the book highlights the societal pain stemming from the erosion of trust, the spread of falsehoods, and the challenges posed to collective cooperation.

Lessons for the Future

a. Resilience and Hope: While unveiling the pain, the book also seeks to uncover stories of hope, resilience, and community solidarity. It explores how communities and individuals have come together, innovated, and found strength in adversity.

b. Opportunities for Growth: By reflecting on the global responses to the pandemic, the book aims to identify lessons learned and opportunities for growth. It serves as a guide for shaping a more resilient, equitable, and compassionate future in the aftermath of the crisis.

In essence, the purpose of "Unveiling Pain" is to provide readers with a holistic and empathetic exploration of the myriad challenges faced by individuals and societies globally during the COVID-19 pandemic. Through this exploration, the book aims to contribute to a collective understanding of our shared humanity and the potential for positive transformation in the wake of adversity.

II. The Human Toll

In the annals of the COVID-19 pandemic, no aspect looms larger or resonates more profoundly than the human toll exacted by the relentless march of the virus. This chapter in "Unveiling Pain: The Global Impact of COVID-19" unearths the deeply personal narratives and collective experiences that define the human cost of this unprecedented global crisis.

Statistics and Stories

a. Global Death Toll: Opening with stark statistics, this section paints a somber picture of the vast number of lives lost to the virus, acknowledging the magnitude of the tragedy.

b. Personal Anecdotes: Interspersed with the numbers are poignant personal stories, offering glimpses into the lives of those directly affected—stories of resilience, loss, and the enduring impact of COVID-19 on families and communities.

Long-term Health Effects

a. Lingering Health Issues: This segment delves into the long-term health effects of COVID-19, exploring the challenges faced by survivors grappling with lingering symptoms and the potential societal implications of a population dealing with post-acute sequelae of the virus.

b. Impact on Healthcare Systems: Examining the strain on healthcare systems, the chapter illuminates the struggles faced by hospitals and healthcare workers in coping with the surge in cases, resource shortages, and the emotional toll of witnessing unprecedented levels of suffering.

Vulnerable Populations

a. Disproportionate Impact: The discussion extends to the disproportionate impact of the virus on vulnerable populations, including the elderly, marginalized communities, and those with pre-existing health conditions. It underscores the systemic inequalities laid bare by the pandemic.

b. Global Health Disparities: The chapter takes a global perspective, shedding light on how different regions faced unique challenges, emphasizing the interconnectedness of health outcomes and the need for collaborative international efforts.

Emotional Resonance

a. Grief and Mourning: Central to this exploration is an examination of the profound grief experienced by individuals and communities. The chapter seeks to capture the emotional resonance of loss, mourning rituals disrupted, and the collective sorrow echoing across nations.

b. Mental Health Struggles: An integral component is the discussion on mental health struggles, acknowledging the toll of isolation, fear, and uncertainty on the psychological well-being of individuals and societies.

Lessons in Humanity

a. Acts of Compassion: Amidst the pain, stories of human compassion and solidarity emerge. This section showcases acts of kindness, resilience, and the indomitable spirit of individuals and communities coming together in the face of adversity.

b. Building a Collective Memory: The chapter concludes by emphasizing the importance of building a collective memory, acknowledging the lives lost, the resilience displayed, and the lessons learned in the crucible of the pandemic. It sets the stage for the subsequent exploration of recovery, healing, and the potential for positive transformation in the wake of immense loss.

In navigating "The Human Toll," this chapter aims to not only document the profound pain experienced but also to honor the resilience and humanity that persists in the face of unprecedented challenges. It serves as a testament to the shared experiences that bind us together as a global community, encouraging reflection, empathy, and a collective commitment to healing.

A. High mortality rates and loss of lives

Section A: High Mortality Rates and Loss of Lives

The opening section of "Unveiling Pain: The Global Impact of COVID-19" begins its exploration by confronting the stark reality of high mortality rates and the profound loss of lives witnessed across the globe. This chapter delves into the heartbreaking statistics and personal narratives that underscore the magnitude of the human toll exacted by the pandemic.

Global Death Toll

a. Statistics and Trends: The section begins with a comprehensive overview of the global death toll, presenting the staggering numbers and trends that underscore the severity of the pandemic's impact on human life.

b. Regional Disparities: Delving deeper, the narrative explores regional disparities, highlighting how certain areas faced more significant challenges in managing the outbreak and, consequently, experienced higher mortality rates.

Personal Narratives

a. Faces Behind the Numbers: Beyond the statistics, the chapter weaves in personal narratives—stories of individuals who succumbed to the virus. These anecdotes serve to humanize the numbers, fostering a connection between the reader and the lived experiences of those affected.

b. Impact on Families and Communities: Examining the ripple effects, the narrative explores how each loss reverberates through families and communities, leaving an indelible mark on the social fabric and collective memory.

Healthcare Struggles

a. Overwhelmed Healthcare Systems: This segment delves into the challenges faced by healthcare systems grappling with an unprecedented surge in cases. It explores the strain on hospitals, healthcare workers, and the ethical dilemmas posed by resource scarcity.

b. Frontline Workers' Stories: Personalizing the healthcare struggle, the chapter incorporates firsthand accounts from frontline workers, shedding light on the emotional toll of providing care in the face of overwhelming circumstances.

Societal Impact

a. Loss of Key Figures: The section addresses the loss of notable figures—leaders, healthcare professionals, and community pillars—and the societal impact of their absence.

b. Interrupted Lives: Exploring how the pandemic disrupted lives at various stages, from the young to the elderly, the narrative underscores the tragedy of potential unrealized, dreams shattered, and futures altered.

Global Grief and Mourning

a. Collective Grief: The chapter culminates in an exploration of the collective grief experienced on a global scale. It examines the challenges of mourning in the context of social distancing measures and the ways in which communities found solace and connection despite physical barriers.

b. Cultural and Religious Practices: Acknowledging the diversity of mourning practices, the narrative highlights how cultural and religious traditions played a role in shaping the grieving process during a time of unprecedented restrictions.

This section serves as a poignant introduction, laying bare the immense loss of life experienced during the COVID-19 pandemic. It sets the stage for the subsequent exploration of the broader impact on health systems, economies, and the social fabric, urging readers to confront the human toll and fostering a deeper understanding of the multifaceted pain etched into the collective memory of our global community.

1. Statistics on global death toll

1.1 Global Death Toll: An Unprecedented Tragedy

The initial chapter of "Unveiling Pain: The Global Impact of COVID-19" begins with a somber examination of the stark statistics surrounding the global death toll caused by the pandemic. This section endeavors to provide readers with a numerical overview of the magnitude of the tragedy, offering a sobering perspective on the profound human toll exacted by the relentless spread of the virus.

Magnitude of Loss

- Raw Numbers: The chapter begins by presenting the raw numbers, encapsulating the sheer scale of lives lost to COVID-19 globally. Statistical data, meticulously compiled from reliable sources, serves as a stark reminder of the magnitude of this global crisis.

- Graphical Representation: Visual aids such as graphs and charts are employed to illustrate trends, trajectories, and the evolution of the death toll over time. This visual representation enhances the impact of the numbers, providing a comprehensive snapshot of the pandemic's trajectory.

REGIONAL DISPARITIES

- Hotspots and Vulnerable Regions: Beyond the aggregate numbers, the narrative dissects regional disparities, emphasizing how certain areas became hotspots for the virus, facing disproportionately high mortality rates. This exploration sheds light on the uneven impact of the pandemic on different communities and nations.

- Factors Influencing Disparities: The text explores the factors contributing to regional variations, such as healthcare infrastructure, socio-economic conditions, and the effectiveness of public health measures. This analysis adds depth to the understanding of why certain regions bore a heavier burden.

Demographic Insights

- Age, Gender, and Pre-existing Conditions: The chapter delves into demographic nuances, examining how age, gender, and pre-existing health conditions influenced mortality rates. This exploration helps elucidate the differential impact of the virus on various demographic groups.

- Vulnerable Populations: Focusing on vulnerable populations, including the elderly and those with underlying health conditions, the narrative emphasizes the heightened susceptibility of certain groups, contributing to a more nuanced understanding of the pandemic's toll.

Implications for Global Health

- Health System Capacities: The section concludes by examining the implications of the global death toll on healthcare systems. It assesses the strain on medical facilities, the challenges faced by healthcare professionals, and the lasting impact on the overall state of global health.

- Long-term Health Disparities: Anticipating the long-term consequences, the chapter briefly touches upon how the pandemic might exacerbate existing health disparities, setting the stage for subsequent discussions on the broader impacts beyond mortality rates.

In narrating the statistics on the global death toll, this section aims to provide readers with a factual and comprehensive foundation for understanding the magnitude of the human tragedy unleashed by COVID-19. It lays the groundwork for the subsequent exploration of personal narratives, societal repercussions, and the multifaceted pain embedded in the wake of unprecedented loss.

2. Personal Stories and Anecdotes: The Human Faces of Loss

As "Unveiling Pain: The Global Impact of COVID-19" delves into the depths of the pandemic's impact, this section brings forth the profoundly personal narratives and poignant anecdotes that breathe life into the statistics. By sharing individual stories, the chapter endeavors to humanize the global tragedy, allowing readers to connect with the lived experiences behind the numbers.

Voices of Loss

- Diverse Perspectives: This segment introduces a diverse array of personal stories, recounting the experiences of individuals who faced the direct impact of COVID-19. Stories cut across demographics, highlighting the universality of the pandemic's reach.

- Geographic Representation: By incorporating stories from various regions and cultures, the narrative emphasizes the global nature of the crisis. Readers encounter the unique struggles faced by people from different corners of the world, fostering empathy and understanding.

Families Torn Apart

● Impact on Families: Through intimate narratives, the chapter explores the profound impact on families torn apart by the loss of loved ones. It delves into the emotional complexities, the struggles of bereaved families, and the lasting void left in the fabric of familial relationships.

● Intergenerational Impact: The stories touch upon the intergenerational impact of the pandemic, examining how the loss of older family members, often pillars of wisdom and guidance, reverberates through younger generations.

Frontline Heroes

● Healthcare Narratives: Personal anecdotes from healthcare professionals on the frontline provide a glimpse into the harrowing experiences of those battling the virus. These stories capture the dedication, sacrifice, and emotional toll experienced by those working tirelessly to save lives.

● Profiles of Resilience: Amidst the challenges, the narrative highlights stories of resilience among healthcare workers, showcasing their determination and the emotional complexities of their dual roles as caregivers and witnesses to immense suffering.

Unfinished Stories

● Interrupted Lives: The chapter addresses the tragedy of unfinished stories—lives cut short by the pandemic. It reflects on the unrealized potential, dreams, and aspirations, exploring the collective mourning for futures altered by the unforeseen consequences of the virus.

● Cultural and Personal Context: Anecdotes are presented within their cultural and personal contexts, providing a nuanced understanding of how diverse communities cope with loss, grieve, and find solace amidst the unprecedented challenges.

Resilience Amidst Loss

● Acts of Kindness: Intertwined with the stories of loss are tales of communities coming together, displaying acts of kindness and support. These narratives emphasize the resilience inherent in the human spirit, even in the face of profound adversity.

● Celebrating Lives: The section concludes by celebrating the lives of those lost, acknowledging their individuality, contributions, and the collective legacy they leave behind. It sets the stage for a broader discussion on healing, remembrance, and the potential for positive transformation.

By infusing the narrative with personal stories and anecdotes, this section aims to evoke an emotional connection with the individuals and families profoundly affected by the pandemic. It serves as a poignant reminder that behind every statistic lies a unique and irreplaceable life, contributing to the tapestry of human experiences during this unprecedented global crisis.

B. Long-term Health Effects: Navigating the Shadows of Uncertainty

In the aftermath of the acute phase of the COVID-19 pandemic, "Unveiling Pain: The Global Impact of COVID-19" turns its focus to the enduring health effects that cast a shadow on the survivors. This section delves into the intricacies of long-term health consequences, exploring the uncertainties and challenges faced by those who have battled the virus.

Lingering Symptoms and Complications

● Post-Acute Sequelae: The chapter begins by introducing the concept of post-acute sequelae of SARS-CoV-2 infection (PASC), commonly known as "long COVID." It explores the range of symptoms that persist beyond the acute phase, from fatigue and respiratory issues to neurological and cardiovascular complications.

● Diverse Manifestations: Highlighting the diversity of long-term symptoms, the narrative draws attention to the multi-system nature of long COVID, emphasizing that its impact extends far beyond the respiratory system.

The Toll on Mental Health

● Psychological Residue: Beyond physical health, the section addresses the profound toll on mental health. It explores how the experience of long COVID contributes to anxiety, depression, and post-traumatic stress, unraveling the layers of psychological distress.

● Challenges in Diagnosis and Treatment: Recognizing the challenges in diagnosing and treating long-term mental health effects, the narrative sheds light on the need for holistic healthcare approaches that address both physical and psychological well-being.

STRAIN ON HEALTHCARE Systems

● Chronic Care Challenges: The chapter examines the strain on healthcare systems posed by the long-term health effects of COVID-19. It delves into the challenges of providing chronic care for individuals with lingering symptoms and the potential impact on healthcare resources.

● Adapting Healthcare Models: The narrative discusses the need for healthcare models to adapt to the long-term nature of some COVID-19 cases, addressing the unique challenges posed by a growing population of individuals with persistent health issues.

Global Health Inequities

● Disparities in Long-Term Outcomes: Exploring the disparities in long-term outcomes, the section considers how factors such as access to healthcare, socio-economic status, and pre-existing conditions may contribute to divergent health trajectories for survivors.

● Global Collaborations for Research: Acknowledging the global nature of long-term health effects, the narrative emphasizes the importance of international collaborations in research and healthcare strategies to better understand and address the varied impacts.

Navigating an Uncertain Future

● Research and Rehabilitation: The chapter concludes by examining ongoing research efforts to understand long-term effects and potential rehabilitation strategies. It emphasizes the collective responsibility to support individuals grappling with lingering symptoms and to contribute to the growing body of knowledge surrounding post-COVID health.

● Patient Advocacy: The narrative underscores the importance of patient advocacy and empowerment, encouraging an inclusive approach that considers the voices of those navigating the uncertain terrain of long-term health effects.

This section aims to shed light on the profound and evolving challenges faced by individuals dealing with the long-term health effects of COVID-19. By navigating the complexities of physical and mental health consequences, the narrative contributes to a more comprehensive understanding of the enduring impact of the pandemic on global health.

1. Overview of Lingering Health Issues: Unraveling the Persistence of COVID-19 Impact

This section of "Unveiling Pain: The Global Impact of COVID-19" embarks on an exploration of the persistent health challenges faced by individuals even after recovering from the acute phase of the virus. By providing an overview of lingering health issues, the chapter aims to unravel the complexity and diversity of post-acute sequelae of SARS-CoV-2 infection (PASC), commonly known as "long COVID."

Post-Acute Sequelae of SARS-CoV-2 (PASC)

• Defining Long COVID: The chapter begins by defining and contextualizing the term "long COVID" or PASC. It elucidates that this condition refers to a range of symptoms that persist for weeks or months after the acute infection has resolved.

• Scope of Symptoms: An overview is provided of the broad spectrum of symptoms associated with long COVID, including but not limited to fatigue, shortness of breath, cognitive difficulties (commonly referred to as "brain fog"), joint pain, and loss of taste or smell.

Multi-System Impact

• Beyond Respiratory System: The narrative emphasizes that the impact of long COVID extends beyond respiratory issues. It explores how the virus can affect multiple organs and systems, including the cardiovascular, neurological, gastrointestinal, and immune systems.

• Complex Interactions: Delving into the complex interactions between the virus and various bodily systems, the section aims to illustrate the intricacies of long COVID and how it defies easy categorization.

Persistent Fatigue and Debilitating Weakness

• Chronic Fatigue Syndrome: The chapter explores the phenomenon of chronic fatigue experienced by many long COVID sufferers. It delves into how this persistent fatigue can be debilitating, affecting the ability to perform daily tasks and disrupting overall quality of life.

• Impact on Daily Functioning: Personal stories and anecdotes are woven into the narrative to illustrate the real-life impact of chronic fatigue, portraying the struggles faced by individuals in their attempts to regain normalcy.

Neurological and Cognitive Impairment

• Cognitive Dysfunction: The narrative addresses the neurological and cognitive impairments associated with long COVID. It explores issues such as difficulty concentrating, memory lapses, and the broader implications for mental well-being.

• Long-Term Consequences: The section delves into the potential long-term consequences of cognitive dysfunction, both in terms of individual experiences and societal implications.

Cardiovascular Complications

• Persistent Heart Issues: Examining the impact on the cardiovascular system, the chapter explores lingering heart issues experienced by some long COVID patients. It discusses conditions such as myocarditis and pericarditis and their implications for long-term health.

• Challenges in Diagnosis: The narrative acknowledges the challenges in diagnosing cardiovascular complications, emphasizing the need for ongoing research to fully understand and address these aspects of long COVID.

Respiratory Challenges and Pulmonary Issues

• Continued Respiratory Symptoms: The section provides insights into how respiratory challenges may persist even after the resolution of the acute respiratory phase. It explores conditions such as shortness of breath, chest pain, and the potential long-term impact on lung function.

• Rehabilitation and Pulmonary Support: The narrative touches upon rehabilitation strategies and pulmonary support for individuals experiencing lingering respiratory issues, emphasizing the importance of multidisciplinary care.

Immunological Conundrums

● Autoimmune Manifestations: The chapter addresses the emergence of autoimmune manifestations as a component of long COVID. It explores the challenges posed by the immune system's response and the potential for prolonged immunological effects.

● Research Frontiers: The narrative highlights ongoing research into the immunological aspects of long COVID, underscoring the complexity of the body's immune response and its implications for long-term health.

By providing an encompassing overview of lingering health issues associated with COVID-19, this section seeks to deepen the reader's understanding of the multifaceted and evolving nature of post-acute sequelae. It sets the stage for a nuanced exploration of the challenges faced by individuals and the imperative for continued research and healthcare strategies to address these persistent health issues.

2. Impact on Individuals and Healthcare Systems: Navigating the Aftermath

This section of "Unveiling Pain: The Global Impact of COVID-19" delves into the far-reaching consequences of the pandemic, exploring the profound impact on both individuals and the healthcare systems that stood at the frontline of the battle against COVID-19.

Individuals' Ongoing Struggles

● Quality of Life Challenges: The chapter begins by delving into the ongoing struggles faced by individuals recovering from COVID-19. It explores how lingering health issues, including fatigue, cognitive impairment, and respiratory challenges, impact their daily lives, relationships, and overall well-being.

● Psychological Toll: Beyond physical health, the narrative addresses the psychological toll on individuals dealing with persistent symptoms. Anxiety, depression, and the uncertainty of long-term health contribute to the complexity of their post-COVID journey.

Challenges in Returning to Normalcy

- Professional and Personal Impact: The chapter navigates the challenges individuals face in returning to normal life. It explores the impact on professional responsibilities, personal relationships, and the adjustments required for those experiencing ongoing health issues.

- Social Stigma: Addressing the potential social stigma associated with long COVID, the narrative sheds light on the importance of fostering understanding and support for individuals navigating the complexities of recovery.

Healthcare System Strain

Overwhelmed Hospitals: The narrative transitions to the strain experienced by healthcare systems. It explores how hospitals were overwhelmed during the acute phase of the pandemic, dealing with surges in COVID-19 cases that stretched resources and capacities to the limit.

- Impact on Healthcare Workers: Delving into the toll on healthcare workers, the chapter examines the physical and emotional exhaustion faced by those on the frontline. Personal stories and anecdotes illustrate the sacrifices made and the resilience displayed by healthcare professionals.

Resource Allocation Challenges

- Scarce Resources: The section addresses the challenges in resource allocation, with a focus on ventilators, ICU beds, and personal protective equipment (PPE). It explores the ethical dilemmas faced by healthcare professionals in deciding how to allocate scarce resources during critical periods.

● Long-Term Implications: The narrative considers the long-term implications of resource scarcity, emphasizing the need for health systems to adapt and enhance resilience in preparation for potential future health crises.

Disruption of Routine Healthcare Services

● Postponed Medical Procedures: The chapter discusses the impact of the pandemic on routine healthcare services, including the postponement of elective surgeries and non-COVID-related medical procedures. It explores how this disruption affected individuals with chronic conditions and non-COVID health needs.

● Backlog and Catch-up Strategies: Addressing the backlog of postponed medical services, the narrative discusses strategies for catching up on delayed healthcare needs and the challenges involved in managing both COVID-19 and non-COVID health demands.

Telemedicine and Technological Adaptations

● Rise of Telemedicine: The narrative explores the accelerated adoption of telemedicine during the pandemic. It considers the positive aspects of this technological shift, such as improved access to healthcare services and the potential for ongoing innovation in healthcare delivery.

● Challenges and Inequalities: Addressing challenges and inequalities associated with telemedicine, the section examines disparities in access to technology, potential limitations in diagnostic capabilities, and the need for a balanced approach to healthcare delivery.

Global Collaborations and Lessons Learned

● International Cooperation: The chapter concludes by highlighting the importance of global collaborations and the exchange of knowledge between nations. It reflects on the lessons learned from the global response to COVID-19 and the imperative for continued cooperation in addressing future health challenges.

● Building Resilient Healthcare Systems: The narrative emphasizes the need for building resilient healthcare systems that can adapt to crises, integrating the lessons learned from the pandemic to enhance preparedness and response capabilities.

By navigating the impact on individuals and healthcare systems, this section aims to provide a comprehensive understanding of the multifaceted challenges faced by both frontline workers and those seeking medical care during and after the acute phase of the COVID-19 pandemic. It sets the stage for further exploration of societal and economic repercussions in subsequent chapters.

III. Economic Fallout

In this chapter of "Unveiling Pain: The Global Impact of COVID-19," the focus shifts to the economic fallout of the pandemic, unraveling the intricate threads of financial impact that have woven through societies worldwide. This section aims to provide a comprehensive exploration of the economic challenges and transformations brought about by the unprecedented disruptions caused by COVID-19.

Global Economic Downturn

- Recessionary Pressures: The chapter commences by addressing the overarching global economic downturn triggered by the pandemic. It delves into the recessionary pressures faced by nations across the world, examining the depth and breadth of the economic contraction.

- Sectoral Impacts: The narrative explores how different sectors, from tourism and hospitality to manufacturing and retail, were disproportionately affected. It sheds light on the interconnectedness of global economies and the ripple effects of disruptions in one sector on others.

Unemployment and Labor Market Challenges

- Soaring Unemployment Rates: The section navigates the soaring unemployment rates witnessed in the wake of lockdowns and economic slowdowns. It considers the impact on diverse segments of the workforce, from blue-collar workers to skilled professionals.

- Shifts in Labor Dynamics: The narrative explores how remote work, digitalization, and shifts in consumer behavior have transformed the labor market. It considers the challenges of reskilling and adapting to new employment paradigms in the wake of the pandemic.

Small Businesses and Entrepreneurship

- Struggles of Small Businesses: The chapter delves into the struggles faced by small businesses, often the lifeblood of local economies. It examines closures, financial stress, and the innovative strategies employed by entrepreneurs to navigate unprecedented challenges.

- Policy Interventions: Addressing government interventions and policies to support small businesses, the narrative explores the effectiveness of relief measures and the broader implications for economic recovery.

Global Supply Chain Disruptions

- Vulnerabilities Exposed: The section examines how the pandemic exposed vulnerabilities in global supply chains. It considers disruptions in manufacturing, logistics, and distribution, and the resulting impact on industries and consumers worldwide.

- Resilience Building: The narrative explores strategies for building more resilient supply chains, emphasizing the need for diversification, technology integration, and risk mitigation in a rapidly changing global landscape.

Government Stimulus and Fiscal Policies

- Unprecedented Stimulus Measures: The chapter discusses the unprecedented fiscal stimulus measures adopted by governments to mitigate economic fallout. It explores the challenges in balancing economic support with long-term fiscal sustainability.

- Global Cooperation: The narrative reflects on international collaborations in economic recovery efforts, considering how nations worked together to stabilize financial markets and support the global economy.

Debt and Austerity Concerns

● Escalation of National Debts: The section delves into the escalation of national debts as governments borrowed extensively to fund relief and recovery measures. It explores concerns related to long-term debt sustainability and potential austerity measures.

● Balancing Fiscal Prudence: Addressing the delicate balance between stimulating economic recovery and ensuring fiscal prudence, the narrative navigates the complexities of post-pandemic economic policymaking.

IMPACT ON GLOBAL TRADE and Investments

● Trade Disruptions: The chapter explores disruptions in global trade, examining the impact of border closures, export restrictions, and shifts in consumer demand on international commerce.

● Investment Trends: The narrative considers the evolving trends in global investments, examining the sectors that attracted capital and the shifts in investor priorities in the aftermath of the pandemic.

Inequality and Social Repercussions

● Widening Economic Disparities: The section addresses the widening economic disparities exacerbated by the pandemic. It explores how vulnerable populations, including low-income workers and marginalized communities, bore a disproportionate burden.

● Social Implications: The narrative considers the social implications of economic inequality, examining its impact on access to education, healthcare, and overall societal well-being.

Opportunities for Economic Transformation

• Innovation and Digitalization: The chapter concludes by exploring opportunities for economic transformation. It reflects on how innovation, digitalization, and sustainable practices can drive economic recovery and pave the way for a more resilient and inclusive global economy.

• Lessons Learned: The narrative emphasizes the importance of learning from the economic fallout, envisioning a future that addresses vulnerabilities, embraces sustainability, and prioritizes equitable economic growth.

By unraveling the economic fallout of COVID-19, this chapter seeks to provide readers with a nuanced understanding of the challenges faced by individuals, businesses, and nations in the wake of the pandemic. It sets the stage for subsequent explorations into the societal, educational, and geopolitical repercussions that have unfolded in the shadow of this global crisis.

A. GLOBAL RECESSION and Economic Downturn

In this section of "Unveiling Pain: The Global Impact of COVID-19," the narrative unravels the profound consequences of the global recession and economic downturn triggered by the pandemic. It delves into the intricate web of financial challenges that have gripped nations worldwide, reshaping economies and reshuffling the deck of global financial stability.

The Specter of Economic Contraction

• Introduction to Recession: The chapter begins by defining and contextualizing the global recession, outlining the key indicators and economic markers that signify a period of contraction. It sets the stage for a comprehensive exploration of the economic landscape in the wake of the pandemic.

● Comparisons with Past Recessions: The narrative draws parallels with historical recessions, providing a backdrop to understand the unique characteristics and challenges posed by the COVID-19-induced economic downturn.

Sectoral Impact and Uneven Resilience

● Disparate Sectoral Challenges: The section explores how different sectors were disproportionately affected by the recession. It delves into the challenges faced by industries such as travel, hospitality, and entertainment, contrasting them with sectors that demonstrated resilience or even growth during the crisis.

● Technological Disruption: Addressing the technological disruptions that played a pivotal role during the recession, the narrative examines how digitalization and remote work became lifelines for certain industries.

Global Trade Disruptions

● Interrupted Supply Chains: The narrative navigates the disruptions in global trade, elucidating how supply chains were severed or severely impacted by border closures, restrictions, and logistical challenges.

● Impact on Export-Dependent Economies: The section explores the economic fallout for nations heavily reliant on exports, as well as the interconnectedness of global trade networks.

Rising Unemployment and Labor Market Strain

● Soaring Unemployment Rates: The chapter addresses the surge in unemployment rates across the globe, examining how widespread business closures and economic contractions led to job losses on an unprecedented scale.

- Labor Market Dynamics: The narrative delves into the complexities of labor market dynamics, exploring the challenges faced by workers in adapting to new employment paradigms and the resilience displayed by those navigating the evolving job landscape.

Government Interventions and Stimulus Measures

- Unprecedented Fiscal Responses: The section explores the fiscal measures adopted by governments to counteract the economic downturn. It examines stimulus packages, monetary policies, and relief efforts aimed at stabilizing economies and supporting individuals and businesses.

- Debt Accumulation and Fiscal Challenges: Addressing the potential long-term consequences of extensive government spending, the narrative considers the implications of rising national debts and the challenges associated with fiscal sustainability.

Impact on Global Investments and Financial Markets

- Volatility in Financial Markets: The narrative navigates the volatility witnessed in global financial markets, examining how uncertainties surrounding the pandemic led to fluctuations in stocks, bonds, and commodities.

- Investment Trends and Strategies: The section explores the changing landscape of global investments, considering shifts in investor priorities, emerging trends, and the implications for long-term economic recovery.

Small Businesses and Economic Resilience

- Struggles of Small Enterprises: The chapter addresses the struggles faced by small businesses, exploring closures, financial stress, and the innovative strategies employed by entrepreneurs to weather the economic storm.

● Role of Government Support: The narrative delves into the role of government support in sustaining small businesses, examining the effectiveness of relief measures and the challenges in balancing economic recovery with fiscal responsibility.

Trade and Geopolitical Ramifications

● Geopolitical Dynamics: The section examines the geopolitical ramifications of the economic downturn, considering how trade tensions, nationalist sentiments, and global power dynamics have been influenced by the financial challenges unleashed by the pandemic.

● Global Cooperation and Diplomacy: The narrative reflects on the need for international collaboration and diplomacy in addressing shared economic challenges and fostering global recovery.

By unraveling the layers of the global recession and economic downturn, this section seeks to provide readers with a profound understanding of the financial turbulence that has characterized the post-pandemic world. It sets the stage for further exploration into the nuanced repercussions on individuals, societies, and the broader geopolitical landscape.

1. Effects on employment and income

This section of "Unveiling Pain: The Global Impact of COVID-19" scrutinizes the far-reaching consequences of the pandemic on employment and income. The narrative delves into the profound shifts in the job market, labor dynamics, and the financial stability of individuals, unraveling the complexities of a world reshaped by unprecedented economic challenges.

Surge in Unemployment

● Unprecedented Job Losses: The chapter begins by outlining the unprecedented scale of job losses triggered by the pandemic. It explores how lockdowns, business closures, and economic contractions resulted in a surge in unemployment, affecting millions across various industries.

• Demographic Disparities: The narrative addresses demographic disparities in unemployment, considering how certain groups, such as young workers, women, and low-skilled laborers, faced heightened vulnerability in the job market.

Shifts in Labor Dynamics

• Remote Work and Digitalization: The section navigates the paradigm shift in labor dynamics, emphasizing the widespread adoption of remote work and digitalization. It explores how technology became a lifeline for certain sectors while posing challenges for others.

• Reskilling and Adaptation: The narrative delves into the necessity for reskilling and adapting to new employment paradigms. It explores how individuals and organizations navigated the evolving job landscape, addressing the need for agility and continuous learning.

Impact on Small Businesses and Entrepreneurs

• Struggles of Small Enterprises: The chapter addresses the challenges faced by small businesses and entrepreneurs, exploring closures, financial stress, and the innovative strategies employed to adapt to the economic downturn.

• Government Support and Policy Measures: The narrative examines the role of government support in sustaining small businesses, considering the effectiveness of relief measures and the challenges in balancing economic recovery with fiscal responsibility.

Income Inequality and Financial Strain

• Widening Income Disparities: The section explores the widening income disparities exacerbated by the pandemic. It delves into how vulnerable populations faced financial strain, examining the challenges of meeting basic needs, such as housing, healthcare, and education.

• Social Implications: The narrative considers the social implications of economic inequality, exploring its impact on access to resources, opportunities, and overall societal well-being.

Job Insecurity and Mental Health

• Psychological Toll of Job Insecurity: The chapter addresses the psychological toll of job insecurity, exploring how uncertainty about employment prospects contributed to anxiety, stress, and mental health challenges.

• Importance of Workplace Support: The narrative reflects on the role of workplace support and mental health initiatives, highlighting the need for organizations to prioritize the well-being of their employees during times of economic uncertainty.

Government Stimulus and Income Support

• Unprecedented Fiscal Responses: The section explores the fiscal measures adopted by governments to provide income support and financial relief. It examines stimulus packages, unemployment benefits, and other initiatives aimed at stabilizing household incomes.

• Debt Accumulation and Long-Term Challenges: Addressing the potential long-term consequences of extensive government spending, the narrative considers the implications of rising national debts and the challenges associated with maintaining sustainable income support.

Global Economic Disruptions and Expatriate Workers

• Impact on Expatriate Workers: The chapter delves into the specific challenges faced by expatriate workers, considering how global economic disruptions and border closures affected the livelihoods of individuals working abroad.

• Repatriation Challenges: The narrative explores the complexities of repatriation, examining the hurdles faced by expatriates in returning to their home countries and the broader implications for global labor markets.

Economic Recovery Strategies

• Employment-Focused Recovery Plans: The section concludes by examining strategies for economic recovery with a focus on employment. It explores initiatives aimed at revitalizing job markets, fostering entrepreneurship, and rebuilding economic resilience.

• Inclusive Growth: The narrative emphasizes the importance of inclusive growth in the recovery process, considering strategies that address income inequality and create opportunities for diverse segments of the population.

By navigating the effects on employment and income, this section aims to provide readers with a nuanced understanding of the profound shifts in the economic landscape brought about by the COVID-19 pandemic. It sets the stage for further exploration into the broader societal and geopolitical repercussions of these economic transformations.

2. Business closures and bankruptcies

In this segment of "Unveiling Pain: The Global Impact of COVID-19," the focus turns to the devastating consequences of widespread business closures and bankruptcies precipitated by the pandemic. The narrative navigates the intricate web of economic disintegration, exploring how enterprises of all sizes grappled with unprecedented challenges, reshaping industries and economies on a global scale.

Epidemic of Business Closures

● Scope and Magnitude: The chapter begins by examining the scope and magnitude of business closures triggered by the pandemic. It explores how lockdowns, supply chain disruptions, and shifts in consumer behavior led to a wave of closures across diverse industries.

● Small Businesses and Local Impact: The narrative considers the impact on small businesses, emphasizing their unique vulnerabilities and the ripple effects on local economies, employment, and community dynamics.

Bankruptcies and Financial Turmoil

● Rise in Corporate Bankruptcies: The section delves into the rise in corporate bankruptcies, exploring how companies across sectors faced financial turmoil. It addresses the complexities of bankruptcy processes and their implications for creditors, employees, and stakeholders.

● Survival Strategies: The narrative examines the survival strategies employed by businesses facing bankruptcy, including debt restructuring, mergers, and acquisitions. It reflects on the evolving nature of business landscapes in the wake of financial crises.

Impact on Industries

● Travel and Hospitality: The chapter navigates the specific challenges faced by industries heavily reliant on travel and hospitality. It examines the struggles of airlines, hotels, and related businesses in the face of travel restrictions and reduced consumer demand.

● Retail and Entertainment: The narrative explores disruptions in the retail and entertainment sectors, addressing the closure of brick-and-mortar stores, cinemas, and entertainment venues. It reflects on the shift towards e-commerce and digital platforms.

Supply Chain Disruptions

● Vulnerabilities in Global Supply Chains: The section addresses vulnerabilities in global supply chains, examining how disruptions in manufacturing, logistics, and distribution contributed to business closures. It reflects on the challenges of mitigating supply chain risks in an interconnected world.

● Localized Production Trends: The narrative explores emerging trends in localized production and supply chain diversification as businesses seek to build resilience in the face of future uncertainties.

Entrepreneurial Resilience and Innovation

● Innovative Responses to Crisis: The chapter delves into the innovative responses of entrepreneurs to navigate the crisis. It explores how businesses pivoted, embraced digitalization, and found creative solutions to sustain operations and adapt to changing consumer preferences.

● Tech and Start-Up Dynamics: The narrative reflects on the dynamics within the technology and start-up sectors, highlighting instances of resilience, adaptability, and the emergence of new opportunities amidst economic challenges.

Government Support and Policy Responses

● Financial Aid and Stimulus Measures: The section examines government support and stimulus measures aimed at preventing widespread business closures. It addresses the effectiveness of financial aid, grants, and policy responses in sustaining businesses during the economic downturn.

● Policy Challenges and Criticisms: The narrative reflects on the challenges and criticisms associated with government policies, considering issues of equity, accessibility, and the unintended consequences of certain relief measures.

Impact on Employment and Local Communities

● Job Losses and Local Economies: The chapter explores the direct link between business closures and job losses, examining how the shuttering of enterprises reverberated through local economies. It considers the social and economic consequences for communities heavily dependent on specific industries.

● Community Resilience and Recovery: The narrative reflects on community resilience and recovery efforts, exploring how local initiatives, support networks, and civic engagement played a role in mitigating the impact of business closures.

Global Economic Transformations

● Shifts in Economic Landscapes: The section concludes by reflecting on the broader transformations in global economic landscapes resulting from widespread business closures. It considers how industries and economies adapt, evolve, and redefine themselves in the aftermath of unprecedented challenges.

● Opportunities for Reinvention: The narrative emphasizes the potential for reinvention and renewal, exploring how the post-pandemic era may witness the emergence of new business models, industries, and economic paradigms.

By unraveling the complexities of business closures and bankruptcies, this section aims to provide readers with a comprehensive understanding of the economic disintegration brought about by the COVID-19 pandemic. It sets the stage for further exploration into the societal, cultural, and geopolitical ramifications of these transformative economic shifts.

IV. Educational Disruption

In this chapter of "Unveiling Pain: The Global Impact of COVID-19," the narrative shifts its focus to the profound disruptions that the pandemic has wrought upon the realm of education. Exploring the multifaceted challenges faced by students, educators, and educational institutions worldwide, this section navigates the complexities of a transformed educational landscape.

Closure of Educational Institutions

- Global Shutdowns: The chapter begins by examining the global closure of educational institutions in response to the pandemic. It delves into how schools, universities, and other learning spaces faced abrupt closures, disrupting traditional modes of teaching and learning.

- Challenges of Remote Learning: The narrative explores the challenges associated with the rapid shift to remote learning, considering issues of technological accessibility, the digital divide, and the adaptability of educators and students to virtual platforms.

Impact on Students

- Disruptions in Learning Continuity: The section addresses how students faced disruptions in the continuity of their education. It explores the varied experiences of learners, from difficulties in adjusting to remote learning to the psychological toll of isolation and uncertainty.

- Educational Inequalities: The narrative examines the exacerbation of educational inequalities, considering disparities in access to technology, quality of internet connectivity, and the availability of conducive learning environments.

Challenges for Educators

• Adaptation to Online Teaching: The chapter delves into the challenges faced by educators in adapting to online teaching methodologies. It explores the learning curve associated with digital tools, the need for professional development, and the innovative approaches employed by teachers.

• Mental and Emotional Strain: The narrative addresses the mental and emotional strain experienced by educators, exploring the pressures of adapting to new teaching modalities, supporting students' emotional well-being, and managing the uncertainties of the educational landscape.

Technological Innovations and EdTech Surge

• Accelerated Adoption of EdTech: The section explores the accelerated adoption of educational technology (EdTech) during the pandemic. It considers how virtual classrooms, online collaboration tools, and other technological innovations became essential components of the educational experience.

• Opportunities and Challenges: The narrative reflects on the opportunities presented by EdTech in enhancing educational accessibility and efficiency while acknowledging the challenges, including issues of digital literacy and concerns about screen time.

Impact on Higher Education

• Shifts in University Dynamics: The chapter addresses the shifts in higher education dynamics, examining how universities adapted to remote learning, dealt with enrollment challenges, and navigated financial uncertainties.

- Global Student Mobility: The narrative explores the impact on global student mobility, considering the challenges faced by international students and the implications for the broader landscape of higher education.

Assessment and Evaluation Challenges

- Changes in Evaluation Practices: The section delves into the challenges associated with assessment and evaluation in remote learning environments. It explores shifts in examination methods, concerns about academic integrity, and the need for alternative evaluation strategies.

- Rethinking Grading Systems: The narrative reflects on the reevaluation of grading systems and the exploration of more holistic approaches to student evaluation in the context of disrupted educational norms.

Societal and Long-Term Implications

- Educational Disparities and Social Impact: The chapter examines the societal implications of educational disruptions, addressing the potential widening of educational disparities and its impact on social mobility and economic equality.

- Long-Term Consequences: The narrative reflects on the long-term consequences of disrupted education, considering how the experiences of students and educators during the pandemic may shape the future of learning, workforce dynamics, and societal structures.

Resilience and Innovation in Education

- Educational Resilience: The section concludes by exploring examples of educational resilience and innovation. It highlights stories of educators, institutions, and communities that demonstrated adaptability and creativity in overcoming the challenges posed by the pandemic.

• The Role of Community Engagement: The narrative emphasizes the importance of community engagement in building educational resilience, fostering collaboration, and ensuring that diverse voices contribute to shaping the future of education.

By unveiling the unprecedented challenges and disruptions in the realm of education, this chapter seeks to provide readers with a comprehensive understanding of the profound impact of the COVID-19 pandemic on learning ecosystems. It sets the stage for further exploration into the broader societal, economic, and cultural transformations influenced by these educational shifts.

A. Closure of schools and universities

In this section of "Unveiling Pain: The Global Impact of COVID-19," the narrative explores the profound disruption caused by the widespread closure of schools and universities in the wake of the pandemic. Examining the challenges faced by students, educators, and educational institutions, this chapter delves into the complexities of a transformed educational landscape.

Abrupt Halt to Onsite Learning

• Global Educational Standstill: The chapter begins by outlining the global phenomenon of abrupt closures of schools and universities. It elucidates how educational institutions around the world were compelled to halt onsite learning, leaving millions of students and educators in a state of uncertainty.

• Impact on Academic Calendar: The narrative addresses the disruptions to the academic calendar, examining how closures affected scheduled exams, graduation ceremonies, and other key milestones in the educational journey.

Transition to Remote Learning

• Rapid Shift to Virtual Platforms: The section explores the rapid transition to remote learning as a response to the closures. It considers how educational institutions, from primary schools to universities, adopted virtual platforms and online tools to continue educational activities.

• Challenges of Remote Education: The narrative delves into the challenges associated with remote learning, including issues of technological accessibility, the digital divide, and the adaptation of curricula to online formats.

Technological Inequalities and the Digital Divide

• Disparities in Access: The chapter addresses the technological inequalities that became starkly evident during the shift to remote education. It explores the digital divide, considering how disparities in access to devices and reliable internet connectivity affected students from different socioeconomic backgrounds.

• Implications for Educational Equity: The narrative reflects on the implications of the digital divide for educational equity, examining how it exacerbated existing disparities in learning opportunities and outcomes.

Educator Adaptability and Support

• Educator Responses to Change: The section delves into the adaptability of educators in the face of unprecedented change. It explores how teachers and professors adjusted their teaching methods, embraced new technologies, and navigated the challenges of remote instruction.

• Need for Professional Development: The narrative addresses the importance of professional development for educators, acknowledging the learning curve associated with virtual teaching and the need for ongoing support.

Student Well-Being and Social Impact

● Psychological Toll on Students: The chapter examines the psychological toll on students caused by the abrupt shift to remote learning. It considers the challenges of isolation, disrupted routines, and the impact on mental health and well-being.

● Social Implications: The narrative reflects on the broader social implications of school and university closures, considering the importance of educational institutions as social hubs and the effects of disrupted social interactions on students' development.

Examinations and Assessment Challenges

● Changes in Examination Practices: The section delves into the challenges associated with examinations and assessments during remote learning. It explores shifts in evaluation methods, concerns about academic integrity, and the need for alternative assessment strategies.

● Innovations in Evaluation: The narrative reflects on the innovations that emerged in evaluation practices, considering the exploration of open-book exams, project-based assessments, and other alternatives to traditional testing.

Innovations in Remote Teaching

● Creative Teaching Approaches: The chapter highlights examples of creative teaching approaches that emerged during the period of remote learning. It explores innovative methods used by educators to engage students, foster collaboration, and create interactive virtual learning experiences.

● Hybrid Models and Blended Learning: The narrative reflects on the potential for hybrid models and blended learning, considering how the experiences of remote education may influence the integration of technology into future educational practices.

Preparing for Future Educational Challenges

Lessons Learned: The section concludes by examining the lessons learned from the closure of schools and universities. It reflects on the importance of preparedness, adaptability, and the role of technology in shaping the future of education.

- Resilience in Educational Systems: The narrative emphasizes the resilience of educational systems and the imperative for ongoing reflection and adaptation to navigate future challenges in the ever-evolving landscape of global education.

By unraveling the disruption caused by the closure of schools and universities, this chapter seeks to provide readers with a comprehensive understanding of the challenges faced by the education sector during the COVID-19 pandemic. It sets the stage for further exploration into the broader societal, economic, and cultural transformations influenced by these educational shifts.

1. Impact on students and educators

This section of "Unveiling Pain: The Global Impact of COVID-19" delves into the multifaceted impact that the pandemic-induced disruptions have had on students and educators worldwide. Examining the challenges, adaptations, and resilience displayed within the educational landscape, the chapter aims to provide a nuanced understanding of the profound consequences experienced by these key stakeholders.

Disruptions in Learning Continuity

- Shift to Remote Learning: The narrative begins by exploring how the abrupt closure of schools and universities necessitated an unprecedented shift to remote learning. It examines the challenges faced by students and educators in adapting to virtual classrooms, online assignments, and asynchronous learning models.

• Varied Access to Technology: The section considers the varied access to technology among students, highlighting the disparities in internet connectivity, device availability, and digital literacy. It reflects on the implications of these disparities for the equitable continuation of education.

Psychological Toll on Students

• Isolation and Uncertainty: The chapter addresses the psychological toll on students caused by the abrupt disruption of traditional learning environments. It explores feelings of isolation, uncertainty about academic futures, and the impact on mental health and well-being.

• Challenges for Vulnerable Populations: The narrative delves into how vulnerable populations, including students from low-income families or those with special education needs, faced unique challenges during the transition to remote learning. It reflects on the efforts to provide inclusive educational support.

Adaptability and Resilience of Educators

• Rapid Transition to Virtual Teaching: The section explores the adaptability and resilience displayed by educators in the face of the sudden shift to remote teaching. It highlights stories of innovative teaching methods, creative use of technology, and the commitment of educators to maintaining educational continuity.

• Balancing Act: The narrative addresses the challenges faced by educators in balancing the demands of remote teaching, managing their own well-being, and navigating the uncertainties of the educational landscape.

Educational Inequalities and Access

• Digital Divide: The chapter delves into the digital divide, examining how disparities in access to technology exacerbated existing educational inequalities. It reflects on the efforts made to bridge this gap, including initiatives to provide devices, internet access, and digital resources to underserved communities.

• Impact on Marginalized Students: The narrative considers the disproportionate impact on marginalized students, exploring how the closure of physical learning spaces affected those who relied on schools for meals, social support, and access to resources.

Assessment Challenges and Academic Integrity

• Changes in Evaluation Practices: The section explores the challenges associated with assessments and examinations during remote learning. It examines shifts in evaluation practices, the implementation of alternative assessment methods, and the considerations for maintaining academic integrity in virtual settings.

• Innovations in Evaluation: The narrative reflects on the innovations that emerged in evaluation practices, considering the exploration of open-book exams, project-based assessments, and other alternatives to traditional testing.

Social Implications and Student Development

• Importance of Social Interaction: The chapter addresses the social implications of disrupted education, considering the importance of peer interactions, extracurricular activities, and the overall impact on the holistic development of students.

• Adapting to New Norms: The narrative explores how students adapted to new norms of socializing, collaborating, and engaging in virtual communities, reflecting on the potential long-term changes in social dynamics.

Support Systems and Community Resilience

● Role of Support Systems: The section delves into the role of support systems, both within educational institutions and communities, in mitigating the impact on students and educators. It explores initiatives to provide mental health support, counseling services, and community-driven educational support.

● Community Resilience: The narrative reflects on instances of community resilience, considering how local initiatives, nonprofit organizations, and grassroots efforts played a role in supporting students and educators during these challenging times.

Future of Education and Lessons Learned

● Lessons for Educational Systems: The chapter concludes by examining the lessons learned from the impact on students and educators. It reflects on the resilience demonstrated by the education sector and the potential for transformative changes in the future of education.

● Adapting for Future Challenges: The narrative emphasizes the importance of adapting educational systems for future challenges, incorporating the lessons learned from the disruptions caused by the pandemic and envisioning a more inclusive, adaptable, and resilient future for education.

By navigating the impact on students and educators, this chapter aims to provide readers with a comprehensive understanding of the human experiences within the educational turmoil triggered by the COVID-19 pandemic. It sets the stage for further exploration into the societal, economic, and cultural transformations influenced by these educational shifts.

2. Digital divide and unequal access to education

In this section of "Unveiling Pain: The Global Impact of COVID-19," the narrative scrutinizes the profound consequences of the digital divide, unraveling how unequal access to technology has magnified educational disparities on a global scale. Examining the challenges faced by students and educators, this chapter navigates the complexities of a world where technological access becomes a determinant of educational equity.

Defining the Digital Divide

- Disparities in Technological Access: The chapter begins by defining the digital divide, outlining the disparities in technological access that emerged during the pandemic. It delves into variations in internet connectivity, device availability, and digital literacy that created a stark divide among students.

- Urban-Rural Disparities: The narrative explores how urban and rural areas experienced distinct challenges, with urban centers often having better access to high-speed internet and technology infrastructure compared to remote or underserved rural regions.

Impact on Remote Learning

- Barriers to Effective Learning: The section examines how the digital divide became a barrier to effective remote learning. It considers challenges such as limited or no access to online classes, difficulties in submitting assignments, and the inability to participate in virtual discussions.

- Exclusion of Marginalized Communities: The narrative addresses how marginalized communities, including low-income households and communities in developing regions, faced heightened exclusion due to the lack of access to essential digital resources.

Varied Access to Devices

- Disparities in Device Ownership: The chapter delves into disparities in device ownership among students. It explores how some students had access to personal computers, laptops, or tablets, while others relied on shared devices within their households or had no access to devices at all.

• Mobile Devices as Educational Tools: The narrative reflects on the role of mobile devices in bridging the digital gap, considering how smartphones became crucial tools for accessing educational content, participating in virtual classes, and completing assignments.

Challenges Faced by Educators

• Technological Proficiency of Educators: The section explores how the digital divide impacted educators, examining the varying levels of technological proficiency among teachers. It addresses the challenges faced by educators in adapting to online teaching and navigating digital platforms.

• Inequities in Professional Development: The narrative reflects on inequities in professional development opportunities for educators, acknowledging the importance of ensuring that teachers receive the necessary training to effectively leverage digital tools for remote instruction.

Government Initiatives and Policy Responses

• Efforts to Bridge the Divide: The chapter examines government initiatives and policy responses aimed at bridging the digital divide. It explores efforts to provide subsidized or free internet access, distribute devices to students in need, and implement strategies for digital inclusion.

• Challenges in Implementation: The narrative reflects on the challenges associated with implementing large-scale initiatives to bridge the digital divide, considering issues of infrastructure, funding, and the need for sustainable, long-term solutions.

Global Perspectives on the Digital Gap

• International Disparities: The section considers the global perspective on the digital gap, examining how different countries faced unique challenges based on their technological infrastructure, economic conditions, and educational systems.

● Collaborative Solutions: The narrative reflects on collaborative efforts between countries, organizations, and tech companies to address global inequalities in access to education. It explores initiatives aimed at providing digital resources to underserved regions and communities.

Innovations in Digital Education

● Emergence of EdTech Solutions: The chapter delves into the emergence of educational technology (EdTech) solutions as a response to the digital divide. It explores innovations in online learning platforms, interactive educational apps, and other tools designed to enhance accessibility and engagement.

● Challenges of Digital Inclusion: The narrative addresses the challenges associated with digital inclusion, considering issues of affordability, cultural relevance, and the need for user-friendly interfaces to ensure that EdTech solutions reach diverse populations.

Long-Term Implications and Educational Equity

● Impact on Educational Equity: The section concludes by reflecting on the long-term implications of the digital divide for educational equity. It considers how addressing technological disparities is pivotal for building a more inclusive and equitable education system.

● The Role of Sustainable Policies: The narrative emphasizes the importance of sustainable policies and ongoing efforts to bridge the digital divide, recognizing that achieving educational equity requires a holistic approach that goes beyond short-term interventions.

By unraveling the challenges posed by the digital divide and unequal access to education, this chapter aims to provide readers with a comprehensive understanding of the educational inequities exacerbated by the COVID-19 pandemic. It sets the stage for further exploration into the societal, economic, and policy implications of addressing these disparities in the post-pandemic era.

B. Future implications for the global workforce

In this section of "Unveiling Pain: The Global Impact of COVID-19," the narrative delves into the far-reaching implications that the pandemic has set in motion for the global workforce. Examining the shifts in employment dynamics, the rise of remote work, and the adaptation of industries, this chapter navigates the evolving landscape that will shape the future world of work.

Acceleration of Remote Work

- Remote Work as the New Norm: The chapter begins by exploring how the pandemic accelerated the adoption of remote work. It reflects on the normalization of telecommuting and the shift in organizational perspectives on flexible work arrangements.

- Technological Infrastructure: The narrative delves into the role of technology in facilitating remote work, addressing the importance of robust digital infrastructure, collaboration tools, and cybersecurity measures in supporting a remote workforce.

Reskilling and Adaptability

- Need for Reskilling: The section examines the increased demand for reskilling and upskilling in response to shifts in job requirements. It explores how individuals and organizations are adapting to new technologies, emerging job roles, and the evolving skill sets needed in a post-pandemic world.

- Importance of Lifelong Learning: The narrative reflects on the importance of a culture of lifelong learning, where continuous education and adaptability become essential for staying relevant in a rapidly changing job market.

JOB MARKET TRANSFORMATIONS

- Dynamic Job Market: The chapter navigates the transformations in the job market, considering the emergence of new industries, the decline of traditional sectors, and the reconfiguration of job roles in response to changing consumer behaviors and global trends.

- Gig Economy Dynamics: The narrative explores the continued rise of the gig economy, examining how freelancing, short-term contracts, and flexible work arrangements contribute to the evolving nature of employment relationships.

GLOBAL ECONOMIC SHIFTS

- Impact on Economic Powerhouses: The section addresses how global economic powerhouses have been affected by the pandemic. It explores the challenges faced by both developed and developing nations, considering the reshaping of economic structures, trade dynamics, and geopolitical considerations.

- Opportunities for Emerging Markets: The narrative reflects on the potential opportunities for emerging markets to redefine their economic roles, foster innovation, and participate in new global value chains.

Organizational Resilience and Innovation

- Adaptive Business Models: The chapter delves into how organizations have had to reassess and adapt their business models for resilience. It explores innovations in supply chain management, digitalization, and sustainability practices as businesses strive to remain agile in the face of future uncertainties.

● Employee-Centric Practices: The narrative addresses the shift towards employee-centric practices, considering the importance of well-being initiatives, flexible policies, and inclusive workplace cultures in attracting and retaining talent.

Public Health and Workplace Safety

● Integration of Health Protocols: The section examines the integration of public health protocols into workplace practices. It considers how organizations are reimagining office layouts, implementing sanitation measures, and adopting health and safety guidelines to ensure the well-being of employees.

● Hybrid Work Models: The narrative reflects on the emergence of hybrid work models that combine remote and onsite work, providing flexibility while maintaining a sense of organizational culture and collaboration.

Economic Disparities and Social Impact

● Widening Income Disparities: The chapter addresses the potential widening of income disparities as a consequence of the pandemic's impact on different sectors of the economy. It explores the social implications of economic inequality and the challenges of fostering inclusive growth.

● Social Responsibility of Corporations: The narrative reflects on the role of corporations in addressing social issues, emphasizing the importance of corporate social responsibility and ethical business practices in mitigating the negative social impact of economic transformations.

Global Collaboration and Workforce Mobility

● Cross-Border Collaboration: The section explores the potential for increased cross-border collaboration in a virtual work environment. It considers how technology facilitates global teamwork and the challenges and opportunities associated with diverse, geographically dispersed teams.

● Implications for Workforce Mobility: The narrative reflects on the implications for workforce mobility, examining how professionals may increasingly choose to work in locations that align with their lifestyle preferences rather than being bound by traditional geographic constraints.

Environmental Sustainability and Green Jobs

● Focus on Sustainability: The chapter delves into the growing emphasis on environmental sustainability in the workforce. It explores the rise of green jobs, the integration of sustainability practices in business operations, and the role of the workforce in advancing a more sustainable future.

● Corporate Sustainability Initiatives: The narrative reflects on corporate sustainability initiatives, considering how businesses are incorporating eco-friendly practices, reducing carbon footprints, and contributing to global efforts to address climate change.

By unraveling the future implications for the global workforce, this chapter aims to provide readers with a comprehensive understanding of the transformative shifts that have been set in motion by the COVID-19 pandemic. It sets the stage for further exploration into the societal, economic, and cultural dimensions of the post-pandemic world of work.

1. Changes in skill requirements

In this segment of "Unveiling Pain: The Global Impact of COVID-19," the narrative delves into the profound shifts in skill requirements driven by the pandemic. Examining the dynamic landscape of the workforce, this chapter explores how the demand for specific skills has evolved in response to global disruptions, technological advancements, and changing work environments.

Digital Literacy and Technological Proficiency

● Essential Digital Skills: The chapter begins by emphasizing the increased importance of digital literacy as a foundational skill. It explores how proficiency in using digital tools, collaborating on online platforms, and adapting to technological changes has become essential across industries.

● Embracing Remote Collaboration Tools: The narrative delves into the specific digital skills required for effective remote collaboration, considering the utilization of video conferencing, project management software, and other virtual communication tools.

Adaptability and Resilience

● Dynamic Adaptation to Change: The section explores the heightened demand for adaptability and resilience. It delves into how individuals and teams need to navigate uncertainty, pivot in response to unexpected challenges, and thrive in environments characterized by rapid change.

● Learning Agility: The narrative reflects on the concept of learning agility— the ability to quickly acquire new skills and knowledge—as a key attribute for professionals navigating the evolving demands of their roles.

Data Literacy and Analysis

● Data-Driven Decision-Making: The chapter addresses the growing significance of data literacy for informed decision-making. It explores how professionals across various sectors need to understand data, interpret analytics, and leverage insights to drive strategic initiatives.

● Emergence of Data-Related Roles: The narrative reflects on the emergence of roles specifically dedicated to data analysis, data science, and business intelligence as organizations increasingly rely on data-driven strategies.

REMOTE WORK COMPETENCIES

• Effective Communication in Virtual Spaces: The section explores the nuances of effective communication in remote work settings. It delves into the importance of clear and concise virtual communication, active listening, and fostering a sense of connection among distributed teams.

• Time Management and Self-Discipline: The narrative addresses the need for strong time management skills and self-discipline in remote work environments. It reflects on strategies for maintaining productivity and work-life balance without the traditional boundaries of a physical office.

Cybersecurity Awareness

• Protecting Digital Assets: The chapter emphasizes the heightened importance of cybersecurity awareness. It explores how individuals within organizations need to be vigilant against cyber threats, protect sensitive information, and contribute to a secure digital environment.

• Roles in Cybersecurity: The narrative reflects on the demand for cybersecurity professionals and the emergence of roles dedicated to ensuring the integrity and security of digital systems.

Soft Skills and Emotional Intelligence

• Emphasis on Soft Skills: The section explores the enduring importance of soft skills, including communication, collaboration, and empathy. It delves into how these interpersonal skills are crucial for building effective teams, managing remote relationships, and fostering a positive work culture.

● Emotional Intelligence in Leadership: The narrative reflects on the role of emotional intelligence in leadership, considering how leaders who demonstrate empathy, resilience, and effective communication contribute to organizational success.

Health and Well-Being Practices

● Prioritizing Employee Well-Being: The chapter addresses the growing emphasis on health and well-being practices in the workplace. It explores how organizations are recognizing the importance of supporting employees' mental and physical health, promoting work-life balance, and fostering a positive workplace culture.

● Mental Health Awareness: The narrative reflects on the need for increased awareness of mental health issues, the destigmatization of seeking support, and the implementation of programs that prioritize the well-being of the workforce.

Cross-Cultural Competence

● Navigating Global Collaboration: The section explores the importance of cross-cultural competence in a globalized and remote work environment. It delves into how individuals and teams can navigate cultural differences, communicate effectively across diverse backgrounds, and foster inclusive workspaces.

● Cultural Intelligence: The narrative reflects on the development of cultural intelligence as a valuable skill, allowing professionals to adapt to different cultural norms and collaborate seamlessly in international settings.

Entrepreneurial Mindset

• Innovative Problem-Solving: The chapter addresses the cultivation of an entrepreneurial mindset. It explores how professionals with an entrepreneurial outlook can contribute to innovative problem-solving, adapt to changing market conditions, and drive organizational success.

• Intrapreneurship in Organizations: The narrative reflects on the concept of intrapreneurship—employees adopting an entrepreneurial approach within a larger organization—and how it contributes to fostering a culture of innovation.

By unraveling the changes in skill requirements, this chapter aims to provide readers with a comprehensive understanding of the evolving competencies demanded by the post-pandemic workforce. It sets the stage for further exploration into the broader societal, economic, and cultural implications of these shifts in the global labor market.

2. Shifting dynamics of education and work

In this section of "Unveiling Pain: The Global Impact of COVID-19," the narrative explores the profound changes in the dynamics of education and work catalyzed by the pandemic. Examining the interconnectedness of learning and professional environments, this chapter navigates the evolving relationships between educational institutions, learners, and the world of work.

Acceleration of Remote Learning

• Remote Education as a Norm: The chapter begins by examining the accelerated adoption of remote learning. It delves into how educational institutions worldwide embraced online platforms, virtual classrooms, and digital resources as a response to the challenges posed by the pandemic.

• Hybrid Learning Models: The narrative explores the emergence of hybrid learning models, where a blend of in-person and remote instruction becomes a flexible and adaptive approach to education.

Integration of Technology in Education

• Digital Transformation in Learning: The section explores the integration of technology in education, considering how digital tools and platforms have become integral to the learning experience. It delves into the role of educational technology (EdTech) in enhancing accessibility, engagement, and personalized learning.

• Innovations in EdTech: The narrative reflects on innovations in EdTech, including virtual reality, augmented reality, and artificial intelligence, as tools that enrich educational content and provide immersive learning experiences.

Lifelong Learning and Continuous Education

• Shift to Lifelong Learning: The chapter addresses the paradigm shift towards lifelong learning. It explores how individuals are increasingly viewing education as a continuous journey, necessitating ongoing skill development and adaptability in the face of evolving industry requirements.

• Micro-Credentials and Online Courses: The narrative reflects on the rise of micro-credentials, online courses, and other flexible learning formats that cater to the needs of a diverse and mobile workforce seeking targeted skill acquisition.

CHANGING ROLE OF EDUCATIONAL Institutions

• Adaptation to Remote Environments: The section explores how educational institutions have had to adapt their structures and methodologies to function in remote and hybrid environments. It delves into the challenges and opportunities faced by traditional educational establishments in meeting the evolving needs of learners.

- Global Collaboration in Education: The narrative reflects on the potential for increased global collaboration among educational institutions, fostering cross-cultural learning experiences and facilitating the exchange of knowledge on a broader scale.

Alignment with Industry Needs

- Collaboration with Employers: The chapter addresses the growing importance of collaboration between educational institutions and employers. It explores how institutions are aligning their curricula with industry needs, offering internships, and providing students with practical, real-world experiences.

- Industry-Recognized Credentials: The narrative reflects on the recognition of industry-specific credentials, certifications, and practical skills as valuable components of an individual's education and employability.

Entrepreneurship and Innovation in Education

- Rise of Entrepreneurial Initiatives: The section explores the rise of entrepreneurial initiatives in education. It delves into how startups and innovative educational platforms have emerged to address gaps in traditional education, offering alternative models and approaches.

- Personalized Learning Pathways: The narrative reflects on the trend towards personalized learning pathways, where individuals have the flexibility to tailor their educational journeys based on their unique goals, interests, and learning styles.

Remote Work as a Catalyst for Education

- Parallel Evolution of Remote Work and Education: The chapter examines the parallel evolution of remote work and education. It explores how the adoption of remote work practices influenced the educational landscape and vice versa.

● Virtual Internships and Work-Based Learning: The narrative reflects on the emergence of virtual internships, work-based learning opportunities, and collaborative projects that bridge the gap between education and real-world work experiences.

Skills for the Future

● Demand for Future-Ready Skills: The section addresses the demand for future-ready skills. It explores how educational programs are evolving to equip learners with a diverse skill set, including critical thinking, creativity, adaptability, and emotional intelligence.

● Integration of Soft Skills: The narrative reflects on the integration of soft skills into educational curricula, acknowledging their significance in preparing individuals for collaborative and dynamic work environments.

Global Talent Mobility

● Impact on International Education: The chapter explores the impact of global talent mobility on international education. It delves into how individuals, motivated by remote work possibilities, may choose educational experiences in different geographic locations without being bound by traditional constraints.

● Cultural Exchange and Diversity: The narrative reflects on the potential for increased cultural exchange and diversity within educational settings as individuals from different parts of the world seek learning experiences that align with their aspirations and career goals.

The Role of Government and Policy

● Policy Responses to Educational Changes: The section examines the role of government and policy in responding to the changing dynamics of education and work. It delves into initiatives to support digital literacy, foster innovation in education, and create an enabling environment for lifelong learning.

- Addressing Educational Inequalities: The narrative reflects on the importance of policies aimed at addressing educational inequalities, ensuring equitable access to quality education, and promoting social mobility.

By unraveling the shifting dynamics of education and work, this chapter aims to provide readers with a comprehensive understanding of the interconnected transformations in learning and professional environments. It sets the stage for further exploration into the societal, economic, and cultural dimensions of a world where the boundaries between education and work are increasingly fluid and adaptive.

V. Mental Health Struggles

Mental Health Struggles: Unmasking the Silent Pandemic Within
In this section of "Unveiling Pain: The Global Impact of COVID-19," the narrative unravels the profound and often overlooked mental health struggles that have emerged as a silent pandemic within the larger crisis. Examining the far-reaching consequences on individuals and communities, this chapter navigates the complexities of mental well-being in the wake of the global upheaval caused by the COVID-19 pandemic.

The Psychological Toll of Uncertainty

- Navigating the Unknown: The chapter begins by exploring the psychological toll of uncertainty. It delves into the challenges individuals face in coping with the unpredictability of the pandemic, including fears about health, economic instability, and an uncertain future.

- Anxiety and Fear Dynamics: The narrative addresses the dynamics of anxiety and fear, examining how the constant barrage of information, coupled with the unpredictability of the virus, has contributed to heightened levels of stress and anxiety worldwide.

Isolation and Its Impact

- Loneliness in Lockdown: The section explores the impact of social isolation during lockdowns. It delves into the challenges of loneliness, reduced social interactions, and the implications for mental well-being, especially for those living alone or separated from loved ones.

- Technological Connections: The narrative reflects on the role of technology in mitigating isolation, examining how virtual connections became a lifeline for maintaining social ties and addressing the emotional toll of physical distancing.

Grief and Loss in a Global Context

- Collective Grieving: The chapter addresses the collective experience of grief on a global scale. It explores the mourning process for lost lives, disrupted routines, and the loss of a sense of normalcy, acknowledging the profound emotional impact on individuals and communities.

- Complicated Grief Dynamics: The narrative reflects on the unique challenges of grieving during a pandemic, where traditional rituals and support systems may be compromised, contributing to complicated grief dynamics.

Economic Strain and Mental Health

- Impact of Financial Uncertainty: The section delves into the mental health implications of economic strain. It explores how financial uncertainties, job losses, and economic downturns have contributed to stress, anxiety, and a sense of hopelessness for individuals and families.

- Access to Mental Health Support: The narrative reflects on the challenges of accessing mental health support in the context of economic strain, considering barriers to care and the need for broader mental health initiatives.

Frontline Workers and Trauma

- Trauma Among Healthcare Professionals: The chapter addresses the mental health struggles faced by frontline workers, particularly healthcare professionals. It explores the trauma, burnout, and emotional exhaustion experienced by those on the front lines of the pandemic.

● Recognition and Support: The narrative reflects on the importance of recognizing the mental health challenges faced by frontline workers and implementing support systems to address their unique needs.

Children and Adolescents

● Impact on Development: The section explores the impact of the pandemic on the mental health of children and adolescents. It delves into the disruptions to routines, social interactions, and educational experiences that may have lasting effects on their psychological well-being.

● Educational Challenges: The narrative reflects on the challenges faced by young individuals in adapting to remote learning, dealing with uncertainty, and coping with the social and emotional aspects of disrupted schooling.

PRE-EXISTING MENTAL Health Conditions

● Exacerbation of Existing Conditions: The chapter addresses the exacerbation of pre-existing mental health conditions. It explores how individuals with conditions such as depression, anxiety disorders, and other mental health challenges faced additional stressors during the pandemic.

● Access to Mental Health Services: The narrative reflects on the importance of maintaining access to mental health services and the challenges posed by disruptions to in-person care during lockdowns.

Stigma and Barriers to Seeking Help

• Addressing Mental Health Stigma: The section explores the persistent stigma associated with mental health issues. It delves into the barriers individuals face in seeking help, including societal stigma, fear of judgment, and the need for broader mental health awareness.

• Promoting Open Conversations: The narrative reflects on the importance of promoting open conversations about mental health, normalizing seeking help, and fostering supportive communities that prioritize emotional well-being.

Resilience, Coping, and Mental Health Resources

• Building Resilience: The chapter emphasizes the resilience displayed by individuals facing mental health struggles. It explores coping mechanisms, adaptive strategies, and the importance of building psychological resilience in the face of adversity.

• Access to Mental Health Resources: The narrative reflects on the need for increased access to mental health resources, including online counseling, helplines, and community-based initiatives that provide support for individuals experiencing mental health challenges.

Global Mental Health Initiatives

• International Collaboration: The section explores global initiatives aimed at addressing mental health on an international scale. It delves into collaborative efforts, research endeavors, and policy initiatives focused on understanding and mitigating the global mental health impact of the pandemic.

• Post-Pandemic Mental Health Strategies: The narrative reflects on the importance of developing comprehensive mental health strategies for the post-pandemic era, acknowledging the enduring impact on mental well-being and the need for sustained support systems.

By unraveling the mental health struggles within the broader context of the pandemic, this chapter aims to provide readers with a compassionate understanding of the challenges faced by individuals and communities worldwide. It sets the stage for further exploration into the societal, economic, and cultural dimensions of building a more resilient and supportive global mental health framework in the aftermath of COVID-19.

A. Isolation and social distancing

In this section of "Unveiling Pain: The Global Impact of COVID-19," the narrative delves into the profound effects of isolation and social distancing measures, shedding light on the emotional and psychological toll exacted on individuals and communities worldwide.

The Paradox of Physical Distance and Emotional Proximity:

● Introduction to Social Distancing: The chapter begins by introducing the concept of social distancing as a public health measure. It explores the paradoxical nature of physical separation coexisting with the innate human need for emotional connection and social bonds.

● The Emotional Vacuum: The narrative delves into the emotional vacuum created by physical isolation, examining the challenges individuals face in navigating a world where the warmth of human interaction is replaced by the cool distance necessitated by the pandemic.

Loneliness as a Silent Pandemic

● Loneliness Amplified: The section explores how social distancing measures have amplified feelings of loneliness. It delves into the psychological impact of prolonged isolation, especially for vulnerable populations, the elderly, and those without a robust social support system.

● Technological Connections and Their Limits: The narrative reflects on the role of technology in mitigating loneliness, acknowledging its ability to bridge physical gaps while recognizing the limitations of virtual connections in fulfilling the nuanced needs of human interaction.

Impact on Mental Health

● Psychological Strain: The chapter addresses the psychological strain induced by isolation. It explores the heightened levels of stress, anxiety, and depression experienced by individuals grappling with the abrupt absence of in-person social interactions and the challenges of adapting to remote work and learning environments.

● Vulnerability of At-Risk Groups: The narrative reflects on the vulnerability of at-risk groups, including those with pre-existing mental health conditions, who may face exacerbated challenges in maintaining mental well-being during extended periods of isolation.

Disruption of Social Rituals and Celebrations

● Missed Milestones and Gatherings: The section explores the disruption of social rituals and celebrations. It delves into the emotional impact of missed milestones, canceled events, and the absence of traditional gatherings that serve as anchors in people's lives.

● Adapting to Virtual Celebrations: The narrative reflects on the adaptation to virtual celebrations and ceremonies, acknowledging both the innovative approaches to maintaining connections and the emotional void left by the absence of shared physical experiences.

Challenges for Families and Relationships

● Strain on Familial Bonds: The chapter addresses the strain on familial bonds due to prolonged proximity and altered routines.

It explores the challenges faced by families in navigating the complexities of shared spaces, remote work and education, and the need for intentional efforts to maintain healthy relationships.

● Impact on Romantic Relationships: The narrative reflects on the unique challenges faced by couples and individuals in romantic relationships, considering the dynamics of physical separation, uncertainty, and the emotional toll of navigating these unprecedented circumstances together.

Economic and Societal Implications

● Impact on Social Fabric: The section examines the broader societal implications of isolation and social distancing. It delves into how the fabric of communities has been altered, with neighborhood interactions, local businesses, and community events undergoing transformations that may have lasting effects.

● Economic Strain and Social Inequality: The narrative reflects on the economic strain experienced by individuals and communities, examining the disparities in the ability to cope with social distancing measures and the potential exacerbation of social inequalities.

Coping Mechanisms and Resilience

● Individual Coping Strategies: The chapter explores the diverse coping mechanisms individuals have employed to navigate the challenges of isolation. It delves into the resilience displayed by people in finding creative outlets, fostering hobbies, and seeking solace in self-care practices.

● Community Support Systems: The narrative reflects on the role of community support systems, including grassroots initiatives, mutual aid networks, and virtual communities that have emerged as sources of connection and solidarity during times of physical separation.

Reintegration Challenges and the New Normal

- Navigating Reintegration Anxiety: The section addresses the anxiety associated with the prospect of reintegration into society. It explores how individuals may grapple with the fear of the unknown, the challenges of readjusting to in-person interactions, and the reshaping of social norms in the post-pandemic world.

- The "New Normal" in Social Interactions: The narrative reflects on the concept of the "new normal" in social interactions, considering how individuals and communities may redefine the boundaries of personal space, hygiene practices, and the meaning of shared experiences in a post-pandemic reality.

By unraveling the complexities of isolation and social distancing, this chapter aims to provide readers with a compassionate understanding of the human toll exacted by these necessary yet challenging measures. It sets the stage for further exploration into the broader societal, economic, and cultural dimensions of rebuilding connections and fostering resilience in the aftermath of the COVID-19 pandemic.

1. IMPACT ON MENTAL well-being

In this segment of "Unveiling Pain: The Global Impact of COVID-19," the narrative explores the multifaceted impact of the pandemic on mental well-being. Examining the emotional fallout on individuals and communities worldwide, this chapter delves into the complex landscape of mental health challenges exacerbated by the global crisis.

Psychological Distress Amid Uncertainty

- Introduction to Psychological Impact: The chapter begins by introducing the psychological distress experienced by individuals amid the uncertainty of the pandemic. It explores the pervasive nature of stress, anxiety, and fear as individuals grapple with the unknowns surrounding health, economic stability, and the future.

● The Toll of Prolonged Crisis: The narrative delves into the cumulative toll of living through a prolonged crisis, considering the compounding effects of ongoing uncertainties, disruptions to daily life, and the persistent threat of the virus.

Heightened Anxiety and Fear Dynamics

● The Anxiety Pandemic: The section explores the prevalence of heightened anxiety as a pervasive aspect of the pandemic's impact on mental health. It delves into the sources of anxiety, including health concerns, economic instability, and the constant influx of information, contributing to a collective sense of fear.

● Navigating Uncertainty: The narrative reflects on the challenges individuals face in navigating uncertainty, examining coping mechanisms, and acknowledging the strain on mental well-being when faced with an ever-evolving crisis.

Depression and the Weight of Isolation

● Loneliness and Depressive Symptoms: The chapter addresses the impact of isolation on mental health, particularly in fostering feelings of loneliness and contributing to depressive symptoms. It explores the emotional weight of social distancing measures and their repercussions on individuals' sense of connection.

● Loss of Social Support: The narrative reflects on the loss of traditional social support systems, considering the absence of physical closeness, reduced in-person interactions, and the challenges of finding solace in a socially distanced world.

Grief and Loss in a Global Context

● Collective Grieving Process: The section examines the collective grieving process experienced on a global scale. It delves into the emotional toll of losing lives, disrupted routines, and the shared sense of loss that has permeated communities worldwide.

• Navigating Complicated Grief: The narrative reflects on the complexities of grieving during a pandemic, where traditional mourning rituals may be altered, and the support systems for coping with loss are reshaped.

Impact on Vulnerable Populations

• Vulnerability of At-Risk Groups: The chapter addresses the heightened vulnerability of at-risk populations, including those with pre-existing mental health conditions, marginalized communities, and individuals facing economic hardships. It explores the unique challenges these groups face in maintaining mental well-being.

• Barriers to Accessing Mental Health Support: The narrative reflects on the barriers individuals from vulnerable populations may encounter in accessing mental health support, including disparities in healthcare resources, stigma, and systemic inequalities.

Frontline Workers and the Burden of Trauma

• Trauma Among Healthcare Professionals: The section explores the mental health struggles faced by frontline workers, particularly healthcare professionals. It delves into the trauma, burnout, and emotional exhaustion experienced by those on the front lines of the pandemic.

• Acknowledging the Emotional Toll: The narrative reflects on the importance of acknowledging and addressing the emotional toll on frontline workers, emphasizing the need for support systems, mental health resources, and destigmatization of seeking help.

Children and Adolescents

● Disruptions to Mental Health Development: The chapter explores the impact of the pandemic on the mental health development of children and adolescents. It delves into the disruptions to routines, social interactions, and educational experiences that may have lasting effects on their psychological well-being.

● Coping Mechanisms and Support: The narrative reflects on the coping mechanisms employed by young individuals and the importance of providing support systems to address the unique challenges they face during these unprecedented times.

Economic Strain and Mental Health

● Stressors of Economic Uncertainty: The section addresses the mental health implications of economic strain. It explores how financial uncertainties, job losses, and economic downturns have contributed to stress, anxiety, and a sense of hopelessness for individuals and families.

● Access to Mental Health Services: The narrative reflects on the challenges of accessing mental health services in the context of economic strain, considering barriers to care and the need for broader mental health initiatives.

Coping Mechanisms and Resilience

● Individual Coping Strategies: The chapter explores the diverse coping mechanisms individuals have employed to navigate the challenges to mental well-being. It delves into the resilience displayed by people in finding creative outlets, fostering hobbies, and seeking solace in self-care practices.

● Community Support Systems: The narrative reflects on the role of community support systems, including grassroots initiatives, mutual aid networks, and virtual communities that have emerged as sources of connection and solidarity during times of emotional hardship.

GLOBAL MENTAL HEALTH Initiatives

- International Collaboration: The section explores global initiatives aimed at addressing mental health on an international scale. It delves into collaborative efforts, research endeavors, and policy initiatives focused on understanding

2. Rise in mental health disorders

In this section of "Unveiling Pain: The Global Impact of COVID-19," the narrative delves into the alarming rise in mental health disorders, examining the factors contributing to the surge in psychological struggles amid the backdrop of the pandemic.

Epidemic Within a Pandemic

- Introduction to the Mental Health Epidemic: The chapter begins by characterizing the surge in mental health disorders as an epidemic within the larger pandemic. It explores the pervasive nature of this crisis, acknowledging that the emotional fallout has become a global health challenge of significant proportions.

- Numbers Tell a Story: The narrative reflects on statistical evidence and data illustrating the rise in mental health disorders, emphasizing the need to move beyond the numbers and understand the human stories behind the statistics.

Anxiety Disorders and the Stress Quotient

- Prevalence of Anxiety Disorders: The section explores the heightened prevalence of anxiety disorders. It delves into the various manifestations of anxiety, from generalized anxiety to specific phobias, and examines how the stress quotient has reached unprecedented levels globally.

● Impact on Daily Functioning: The narrative reflects on the impact of anxiety disorders on daily functioning, relationships, and overall quality of life, considering the challenges individuals face in navigating heightened states of worry and fear.

Depression as a Silent Pandemic

● Widespread Increase in Depression Rates: The chapter addresses the silent pandemic of depression, acknowledging the widespread increase in depression rates worldwide. It explores the multifaceted nature of depressive symptoms and their implications for individuals and communities.

● Hidden Struggles: The narrative reflects on the hidden struggles associated with depression, emphasizing the need to destigmatize mental health conversations and create an environment where individuals feel empowered to seek help.

Post-Traumatic Stress Disorders (PTSD)

● Emergence of PTSD Cases: The section examines the emergence of post-traumatic stress disorders (PTSD) in the aftermath of the pandemic's various shocks. It delves into how traumatic experiences, such as loss, isolation, or frontline work, may contribute to the development of PTSD.

● Long-Term Implications: The narrative reflects on the potential long-term implications of PTSD, considering its impact on individuals' mental well-being and the need for tailored therapeutic interventions.

Substance Use Disorders as Coping Mechanisms

● Escalation of Substance Use: The chapter addresses the escalation of substance use disorders as coping mechanisms. It explores how individuals, facing unprecedented stressors, may turn to substances as a means of self-medication and escape.

● Interconnected Nature of Mental Health and Substance Use: The narrative reflects on the interconnected nature of mental health and substance use disorders, emphasizing the importance of holistic approaches to treatment and support.

Suicidal Ideation and Self-Harm

● Rising Cases of Suicidal Ideation: The section delves into the rising cases of suicidal ideation and self-harm. It explores the intricate web of factors contributing to individuals contemplating self-harm or suicide, highlighting the urgent need for mental health interventions.

● Preventive Strategies: The narrative reflects on preventive strategies, including increased awareness, accessible mental health services, and community support, as crucial components in addressing the risk of suicidal ideation.

IMPACT ON CHILDREN and Adolescents

● Surge in Youth Mental Health Disorders: The chapter explores the surge in mental health disorders among children and adolescents. It delves into the unique challenges faced by young individuals, from disruptions to education and social interactions to the pervasive influence of digital environments.

● Early Intervention and Support: The narrative reflects on the importance of early intervention and support systems for youth mental health, emphasizing the role of educational institutions, families, and communities in fostering resilience among young individuals.

Impact on Gender-Specific Mental Health

● Gender Disparities in Mental Health Impact: The section addresses gender-specific disparities in the impact of mental health struggles. It explores how societal expectations, economic pressures, and caregiving responsibilities may contribute to distinct challenges for individuals based on gender.

● Intersectionality and Mental Health: The narrative reflects on the intersectionality of mental health challenges, considering how factors such as race, socio-economic status, and gender identity intersect to shape individuals' experiences of psychological struggles.

Access Barriers to Mental Health Services

● Increasing Disparities in Access: The chapter examines the increasing disparities in access to mental health services. It delves into barriers such as financial constraints, lack of awareness, and systemic inequalities that hinder individuals from seeking and receiving timely mental health support.

● Telehealth as a Double-Edged Sword: The narrative reflects on the role of telehealth in addressing access barriers, acknowledging its potential benefits while also recognizing challenges related to digital divides and equitable healthcare delivery.

Global Collaborative Efforts to Address the Mental Health Surge

● International Response and Collaboration: The section explores global collaborative efforts aimed at addressing the surge in mental health disorders. It delves into initiatives, research endeavors, and policy frameworks developed at the international level to understand, prevent, and treat mental health challenges on a global scale.

- The Imperative for Comprehensive Mental Health Strategies: The narrative reflects on the imperative for comprehensive mental health strategies, emphasizing the need for sustained efforts to destigmatize mental health, increase awareness, and provide accessible and inclusive mental health services for all.

By unraveling the rise in mental health disorders, this chapter aims to provide readers with a comprehensive understanding of the pervasive and interconnected challenges faced by individuals and communities. It sets the stage for further exploration into the societal, economic, and cultural dimensions of building a more resilient and supportive global mental health framework in the aftermath of the COVID-19 pandemic.

VI. Strain on Healthcare Systems

In this section of "Unveiling Pain: The Global Impact of COVID-19," the narrative delves into the unprecedented strain placed on healthcare systems worldwide, examining the multifaceted challenges faced by healthcare professionals, institutions, and infrastructure in the crucible of the pandemic.

Introduction to Healthcare System Strain

- Defining the Unprecedented Challenge: The chapter opens by defining the unprecedented challenge faced by healthcare systems globally. It explores how the rapid spread of COVID-19 overwhelmed the capacity of healthcare infrastructure, leading to a crisis that transcended national borders.

- The Crucible of Crisis: The narrative establishes the healthcare system as the crucible of crisis, where the demands for medical care, resources, and personnel surged to levels unforeseen in modern times.

Overwhelmed Medical Facilities

- Capacity Exceedance: The section addresses the overwhelming number of medical facilities, from hospitals to clinics, as the sheer volume of COVID-19 cases strained the available beds, equipment, and healthcare personnel.

- Field Hospitals and Temporary Solutions: The narrative reflects on the innovative measures taken, including the establishment of field hospitals and repurposing of facilities, to accommodate the influx of patients and adapt to the evolving demands of the crisis.

Shortages in Critical Medical Supplies

- PPE Shortages: The chapter explores the critical shortages in personal protective equipment (PPE), a defining aspect of the early stages of the pandemic. It delves into the global scramble for essential supplies and the impact on the safety of healthcare workers.

- Ventilator Scarcity: The narrative addresses the scarcity of ventilators, highlighting how the surge in severe cases strained the availability of life-saving equipment and prompted rapid responses from manufacturers and governments.

Healthcare Workforce Burnout

- Emotional Toll on Healthcare Professionals: The section examines the emotional toll on healthcare professionals, from doctors and nurses to support staff, as they grappled with the unrelenting demands, long hours, and the emotional strain of witnessing widespread suffering.

- Burnout and Mental Health Challenges: The narrative reflects on the prevalence of burnout and mental health challenges among healthcare workers, acknowledging the need for support systems and interventions to address the unique pressures they faced.

Logistical Challenges in Vaccine Distribution

- Vaccine Rollout Struggles: The chapter addresses the logistical challenges in the distribution of vaccines, from supply chain complexities to equitable access. It explores the race to vaccinate populations amid global demand and the hurdles faced by healthcare systems in implementing mass vaccination campaigns.

- Global Disparities in Vaccine Access: The narrative reflects on the global disparities in vaccine access, considering the challenges of ensuring equitable distribution, particularly for low-income countries with limited resources.

Strain on Non-COVID-19 Healthcare Services

● Disruptions to Routine Healthcare: The section explores the strain on non-COVID-19 healthcare services, as resources were diverted, and routine medical procedures, screenings, and treatments were delayed or disrupted.

● Impact on Chronic Disease Management: The narrative reflects on the repercussions for individuals managing chronic conditions, acknowledging the challenges of accessing regular care and the potential long-term health consequences.

Financial Strain on Healthcare Institutions

● Economic Impact on Hospitals: The chapter addresses the financial strain on healthcare institutions, from increased expenses for COVID-19 response to revenue loss from canceled elective procedures. It explores the economic challenges faced by hospitals, clinics, and healthcare systems globally.

● Need for Healthcare Infrastructure Investment: The narrative reflects on the need for sustained investment in healthcare infrastructure to enhance resilience and preparedness for future global health crises.

Global Disparities in Healthcare Capacity

● Challenges in Developing Regions: The section examines global disparities in healthcare capacity, emphasizing the challenges faced by developing regions with limited resources. It explores how the pandemic exposed and exacerbated existing healthcare inequalities.

● Call for International Collaboration: The narrative reflects on the imperative for international collaboration in strengthening healthcare systems, sharing knowledge, and building capacity to address global health challenges collectively.

Lessons Learned and Calls for Reform

● Reflection on Pandemic Response: The chapter reflects on the lessons learned from the pandemic response, considering both successes and shortcomings. It explores the necessity for adaptive strategies, preparedness, and a renewed focus on public health infrastructure.

● Calls for Healthcare System Reform: The narrative acknowledges the calls for reform in healthcare systems worldwide, emphasizing the need for a more resilient, equitable, and patient-centric approach to healthcare delivery.

Community Engagement in Healthcare Resilience

● Role of Communities in Healthcare Resilience: The section explores the role of communities in healthcare resilience. It delves into the importance of community engagement, public health education, and the collective responsibility in supporting healthcare systems during crises.

● Building a Culture of Preparedness: The narrative reflects on the necessity of building a culture of preparedness within communities, where individuals actively contribute to public health measures, support healthcare workers, and advocate for policies that strengthen healthcare infrastructure.

By unraveling the strain on healthcare systems, this chapter aims to provide readers with a comprehensive understanding of the challenges faced by healthcare professionals and institutions during the COVID-19 pandemic. It sets the stage for further exploration into the societal, economic, and cultural dimensions of rebuilding and reforming global healthcare systems in the aftermath of this unprecedented crisis.

A. Overwhelmed hospitals and healthcare workers

In this section of "Unveiling Pain: The Global Impact of COVID-19," the narrative delves into the critical issue of overwhelmed hospitals and the tireless struggles faced by healthcare workers on the frontline of the pandemic. This chapter unfolds the intense challenges, emotional toll, and resilience displayed by those at the forefront of the battle against COVID-19.

Introduction to the Frontline Battle

- Defining the Frontline: The chapter opens by defining the frontline in the battle against COVID-19, emphasizing hospitals and healthcare workers as the vanguards in confronting the unprecedented challenges posed by the pandemic.

- The Human Cost: The narrative establishes the human cost associated with overwhelmed hospitals, illustrating the toll on both healthcare professionals and the individuals seeking care.

Capacity Exceedance in Medical Facilities

- Surge in Patient Admissions: The section addresses the surge in patient admissions that overwhelmed hospitals globally. It explores how the sudden influx of COVID-19 cases strained the capacity of medical facilities, leading to shortages in beds, equipment, and personnel.

- Field Hospitals and Temporary Solutions: The narrative reflects on the deployment of field hospitals and other temporary solutions to expand capacity, providing insights into the innovative measures adopted to address the crisis.

Shortages in Personal Protective Equipment (PPE)

- Critical Importance of PPE: The chapter explores the critical shortage of personal protective equipment (PPE) as a defining challenge for frontline healthcare workers. It delves into the initial struggles to secure adequate supplies to ensure the safety of those on the frontline.

● Risks and Sacrifices: The narrative reflects on the risks and sacrifices made by healthcare workers when faced with PPE shortages, highlighting the ethical dilemmas and difficult decisions they encountered.

Emotional Toll on Healthcare Professionals

Mental Health Struggles: The section addresses the emotional toll on healthcare professionals, examining the mental health struggles faced by those on the frontline. It explores the stress, anxiety, and trauma experienced as they grappled with the scale and intensity of the pandemic.

● Burnout and Compassion Fatigue: The narrative reflects on the pervasive burnout and compassion fatigue among healthcare workers, acknowledging the toll on their well-being and the urgent need for support systems.

Challenges in Maintaining Standard of Care

● Adaptation to Crisis Standards: The chapter explores the challenges faced in maintaining the standard of care amid the overwhelming patient load. It delves into the ethical considerations and difficult decisions made by healthcare professionals as they adapted to crisis standards.

● Impact on Patient Outcomes: The narrative reflects on the impact of overwhelmed hospitals on patient outcomes, considering the complexities of providing quality care in crisis situations.

Global Collaboration and Resource Sharing

● International Support Networks: The section examines the importance of global collaboration and resource sharing. It delves into how nations and healthcare institutions collaborated to share knowledge, expertise, and resources in the face of overwhelming challenges.

- Lessons Learned from International Cooperation: The narrative reflects on the lessons learned from international cooperation, emphasizing the need for continued collaboration in building a more resilient global healthcare infrastructure.

Innovative Solutions and Technological Integration

- Telemedicine and Remote Care: The chapter addresses the role of innovative solutions and technological integration in alleviating the strain on hospitals. It explores the rapid adoption of telemedicine and remote care to provide essential services while minimizing in-person interactions.

- Challenges and Opportunities: The narrative reflects on the challenges and opportunities presented by the integration of technology, acknowledging the potential for transforming healthcare delivery in the post-pandemic era.

Mobilization of Retired and Volunteer Healthcare Workers

- Call to Action: The section explores the mobilization of retired and volunteer healthcare workers in response to the overwhelming demand. It delves into the call to action that saw healthcare professionals coming out of retirement and volunteers stepping up to support overwhelmed hospitals.

- Community Solidarity: The narrative reflects on the solidarity within communities, as individuals with healthcare expertise contributed their skills to the collective effort in combating the pandemic.

Impact on Training and Education

• Disruptions to Medical Education: The chapter addresses the disruptions to medical education and training caused by overwhelmed hospitals. It explores how the pandemic altered the traditional pathways for medical students and residents, impacting their learning experiences.

• Adaptations in Healthcare Education: The narrative reflects on the adaptations made in healthcare education, acknowledging the resilience of future healthcare professionals as they navigated the challenges posed by the pandemic.

Recognition and Appreciation for Healthcare Workers

• Global Acknowledgment: The section examines the global acknowledgment and appreciation for healthcare workers. It delves into the various initiatives, from applause and tributes to policy changes, aimed at recognizing the dedication and sacrifices of those on the frontline.

• The Need for Sustained Support: The narrative reflects on the importance of sustained support and recognition for healthcare workers, emphasizing the enduring impact of their contributions and the need for continued efforts to prioritize their well-being.

By unraveling the overwhelming challenges faced by hospitals and healthcare workers, this chapter aims to provide readers with a profound understanding of the sacrifices, resilience, and collaborative spirit displayed by those at the forefront of the COVID-19 pandemic. It sets the stage for further exploration into the societal, economic, and cultural dimensions of rebuilding and fortifying global healthcare systems in the aftermath of this unprecedented crisis.

1. Stories from frontline workers

In this segment of "Unveiling Pain: The Global Impact of COVID-19," the narrative brings to light the poignant stories of frontline workers—individuals who stood at the epicenter of the pandemic, facing unparalleled challenges with courage, resilience, and unwavering compassion.

The Nurse's Diary: A Chronicle of Compassion

● Introduction to Frontline Narratives: The chapter opens with a collection of diary entries from a dedicated nurse working on the frontlines. These entries provide an intimate portrayal of daily challenges, emotional triumphs, and the profound impact of caring for COVID-19 patients.

● Navigating Emotional Turmoil: The narrative explores the emotional turmoil faced by the nurse, ranging from moments of heartbreak to instances of joy and connection amidst the chaos. It sheds light on the resilience required to navigate the emotional rollercoaster of frontline healthcare.

The Doctor's Odyssey: Balancing Hope and Despair

● Portrait of a Physician's Journey: The section delves into the journey of a frontline doctor, illustrating the delicate balance between instilling hope and confronting the harsh realities of the pandemic. It explores the doctor's personal reflections on the evolving landscape of patient care.

● Tough Choices and Ethical Dilemmas: The narrative reflects on the tough choices and ethical dilemmas faced by the doctor, emphasizing the complexities of decision-making in a high-stakes medical environment.

The Paramedic's Call to Duty: Answering Urgent Needs

● Day in the Life of a Paramedic: This part provides a glimpse into the life of a paramedic responding to emergency calls during the pandemic. It illuminates the challenges faced on the frontlines of pre-hospital care and the urgency of their role in the overall healthcare system.

- Adaptability and Quick Thinking: The narrative explores the adaptability and quick thinking required of paramedics, highlighting the critical role they played in the swift response to COVID-19 emergencies.

The Unsung Heroes: Support Staff Perspectives

- Voices of Support Staff: This section amplifies the voices of support staff—janitors, administrative personnel, and other essential workers—whose contributions often go unnoticed. It sheds light on their indispensable role in maintaining the functionality of overwhelmed hospitals.

- Resilience in Essential Roles: The narrative reflects on the resilience displayed by support staff, showcasing their dedication to keeping healthcare facilities running smoothly despite the challenges posed by the pandemic.

Community Engagement: Volunteers on the Frontlines

- Stories of Volunteerism: The chapter features stories of volunteers who stepped up to support overwhelmed hospitals. It explores the diverse backgrounds and motivations of individuals who volunteered their time and skills to assist healthcare workers.

- Impact Beyond the Hospital Walls: The narrative reflects on the broader impact of community engagement, acknowledging the ripple effect of volunteer efforts in supporting both frontline workers and the communities they served.

A TALE OF COLLABORATION: International Healthcare Teams

- Global Collaborative Endeavors: This part unfolds narratives of international healthcare teams working together to combat the global crisis. It highlights stories of collaboration, knowledge sharing, and mutual support across borders.

• Lessons Learned from Global Partnerships: The narrative reflects on the lessons learned from international collaboration, emphasizing the significance of shared experiences and the collective strength of a united global healthcare community.

In Memoriam: Remembering Fallen Heroes

• Tributes to Fallen Healthcare Workers: The chapter pays tribute to healthcare workers who lost their lives in the line of duty. It shares stories of courage, sacrifice, and the enduring impact of those who made the ultimate sacrifice in the fight against COVID-19.

• Legacy of Compassion: The narrative reflects on the enduring legacy of fallen healthcare heroes, acknowledging their contributions and underscoring the importance of honoring their memory.

Voices of Hope: Success Stories and Triumphs

• Celebrating Successes: This section highlights success stories and triumphs experienced by frontline workers. It celebrates moments of recovery, resilience, and the indomitable human spirit that persevered in the face of adversity.

• Messages of Hope: The narrative reflects on the messages of hope emanating from frontline success stories, emphasizing the power of human connection, innovation, and collective determination to overcome challenges.

By bringing forth the stories of frontline workers, this chapter aims to humanize the experiences, sacrifices, and triumphs of those who played a pivotal role in confronting the global impact of COVID-19. These narratives provide a personal and poignant lens through which readers can appreciate the profound humanity that unfolded amidst the pain and challenges of the pandemic.

2. Struggles with resource allocation

This section of "Unveiling Pain: The Global Impact of COVID-19" delves into the intricate challenges faced by healthcare institutions and policymakers in managing the allocation of critical resources during the pandemic. The narratives shed light on the ethical dilemmas, tough decisions, and resilience exhibited in the face of resource scarcity.

Introduction to Resource Allocation Dilemmas

- Defining the Resource Balancing Act: The chapter opens by defining the resource balancing act that became a central challenge during the pandemic. It explores the unprecedented demand for medical resources, from ventilators and ICU beds to life-saving medications, and the ethical complexities of distributing them equitably.

- The Human Impact: The narrative emphasizes the human impact of resource allocation decisions, highlighting the lives affected by the scarcity of essential medical supplies and services.

The Ventilator Quandary: Deciding Who Gets Priority

- Ethical Dilemmas in Ventilator Allocation: This part delves into the ethical dilemmas faced in allocating ventilators, a critical resource in treating severe COVID-19 cases. It explores the decision-making processes, criteria, and the emotional toll on healthcare professionals.

- Stories of Ventilator Prioritization: The narrative shares stories of hospitals and healthcare workers grappling with ventilator prioritization, providing a nuanced understanding of the challenges involved.

Scarcity of Personal Protective Equipment (PPE): Safeguarding Protectors

● Critical Importance of PPE: The section addresses the scarcity of personal protective equipment (PPE) and the challenges in safeguarding healthcare workers. It explores stories of hospitals facing shortages and the improvisations made to ensure frontline safety.

● Innovative Solutions: The narrative reflects on innovative solutions adopted to address PPE shortages, from community-driven initiatives to the adaptation of manufacturing processes to meet demand.

Triage and Bed Allocation: Navigating Limited Spaces

● Dilemmas in Triage Protocols: This part explores the dilemmas faced in implementing triage protocols to allocate scarce resources, including ICU beds. It examines the ethical considerations, societal implications, and emotional toll on healthcare providers.

● Strategic Decision-Making: The narrative reflects on the strategic decision-making processes involved in bed allocation, acknowledging the need for transparency, fairness, and adaptability in evolving healthcare landscapes.

Medication Shortages: Navigating Pharmaceutical Constraints

● Impact of Medication Scarcity: The chapter addresses the impact of medication shortages, particularly drugs critical for COVID-19 treatment. It explores the challenges faced by healthcare professionals in ensuring a steady supply of essential pharmaceuticals.

● Global Cooperation in Pharmaceutical Production: The narrative reflects on global efforts to address medication shortages, emphasizing the importance of international collaboration in pharmaceutical production and distribution.

Strategic Planning and Adaptive Responses: Building Resilience

● Strategies for Resource Optimization: This section explores the strategic planning undertaken by healthcare institutions to optimize resources. It delves into adaptive responses, scenario planning, and lessons learned from the dynamic nature of the pandemic.

● Building Resilience for Future Challenges: The narrative reflects on the importance of building resilience in healthcare systems, emphasizing the need for ongoing strategic planning, investment in infrastructure, and global cooperation to prepare for future challenges.

Community Engagement in Resource Support: Mobilizing Solidarity

● Role of Communities in Resource Support: This part illuminates the role of communities in supporting healthcare institutions during times of resource scarcity. It explores stories of community-driven initiatives, donations, and volunteer efforts to bridge gaps in essential resources.

● Collective Solidarity: The narrative reflects on the collective solidarity demonstrated by communities, emphasizing the symbiotic relationship between healthcare institutions and the populations they serve.

Policies and Governance: Navigating Uncharted Territory

● Governmental Decision-Making: The chapter addresses the role of policies and governance in navigating the challenges of resource allocation. It explores how governments and regulatory bodies made decisions to guide healthcare institutions through uncharted territory.

● Lessons Learned in Policy Formulation: The narrative reflects on the lessons learned in policy formulation, emphasizing the need for adaptable frameworks and evidence-based decision-making in addressing resource allocation dilemmas.

Transparency and Communication: Managing Expectations

● Importance of Transparent Communication: This section explores the importance of transparent communication in managing public expectations during resource scarcity. It delves into stories of healthcare institutions striving to maintain open communication channels to foster understanding.

● Mitigating Fear and Uncertainty: The narrative reflects on the role of transparent communication in mitigating fear and uncertainty, emphasizing the need for honesty and empathy in conveying the complexities of resource allocation.

Post-Pandemic Reflections: Learning for Future Preparedness

● Reflecting on Resource Allocation Challenges: The chapter concludes by reflecting on the resource allocation challenges faced during the pandemic. It explores how these challenges have informed discussions on future preparedness, emphasizing the importance of global collaboration, investment in healthcare infrastructure, and ethical considerations in resource allocation planning.

● Building a Resilient Future: The narrative reflects on the collective learnings from resource allocation challenges, underscoring the imperative for building a resilient and equitable healthcare future that can withstand unforeseen global health crises.

By delving into the struggles with resource allocation, this chapter aims to provide readers with a profound understanding of the ethical, logistical, and emotional dimensions involved in managing critical resources during a global health crisis. It sets the stage for further exploration into the societal, economic, and cultural dimensions of rebuilding and reforming global healthcare systems in the aftermath of the COVID-19 pandemic.

B. Global vaccine distribution challenges

This section of "Unveiling Pain: The Global Impact of COVID-19" unravels the complexities and challenges associated with the global distribution of vaccines. It sheds light on the intricacies of ensuring equitable access to COVID-19 vaccines on a worldwide scale, exploring the hurdles faced by nations, organizations, and communities in their quest for widespread immunization.

Introduction to Global Vaccine Distribution Dilemmas

- Defining the Global Challenge: The chapter opens by defining the global challenge of distributing COVID-19 vaccines. It explores the unprecedented scale and urgency of vaccination efforts, emphasizing the need for equitable access to immunization as a key component in overcoming the pandemic.

- The Stakes of Unequal Access: The narrative underscores the stakes of unequal access to vaccines, considering the potential for prolonged suffering, economic disparities, and the perpetuation of the global health crisis.

Vaccine Nationalism and Hoarding: The Race for Doses

- The Phenomenon of Vaccine Nationalism: This part delves into the phenomenon of vaccine nationalism, exploring how some nations prioritized securing doses for their populations, potentially hindering global efforts for equitable distribution.

- Impacts on Global Cooperation: The narrative reflects on the impacts of vaccine hoarding on global cooperation, emphasizing the need for collaborative strategies to ensure fair access for all.

Supply Chain Bottlenecks: From Production to Delivery

● Challenges in Vaccine Production: The chapter addresses challenges in vaccine production, from securing raw materials to ensuring efficient manufacturing processes. It explores the bottlenecks that affected the global supply chain and constrained the availability of doses.

● Logistical Hurdles in Distribution: The narrative reflects on logistical hurdles in vaccine distribution, considering the complexities of transporting, storing, and administering vaccines, particularly those with specific temperature requirements.

The Dilemma of Vaccine Hesitancy: Navigating Public Perception

● Understanding Vaccine Hesitancy: This section explores the dilemma of vaccine hesitancy, examining the challenges in persuading individuals to accept the vaccine. It considers cultural, social, and political factors influencing public perception.

● Communication Strategies: The narrative reflects on communication strategies employed to address vaccine hesitancy, emphasizing the importance of transparent and culturally sensitive messaging to build public trust.

Equitable Access for Developing Nations: Bridging the Divide

● Disparities in Vaccine Access: The chapter addresses disparities in vaccine access, particularly for developing nations with limited resources. It explores the efforts made by global organizations and governments to bridge the divide and ensure that vulnerable populations receive timely immunization.

● The Role of International Collaboration: The narrative reflects on the role of international collaboration in facilitating equitable vaccine access, highlighting initiatives such as COVAX and partnerships between developed and developing nations.

Intellectual Property and Patent Challenges: Balancing Innovation and Access

- Debates on Intellectual Property: This part delves into debates surrounding intellectual property and vaccine patents, exploring how these discussions influenced vaccine availability. It examines the balance between protecting innovation and ensuring broad access to life-saving vaccines.

- Calls for Technology Transfer: The narrative reflects on calls for technology transfer and the sharing of vaccine-related knowledge, emphasizing the potential impact on increasing production capacity globally.

Vaccine Diplomacy: Geopolitical Influences on Distribution

- Geopolitical Considerations: The chapter addresses the influences of geopolitics on vaccine distribution, exploring instances of vaccine diplomacy and the strategic positioning of nations in the global arena.

- Impacts on International Relations: The narrative reflects on the impacts of vaccine diplomacy on international relations, considering both cooperative and competitive dynamics in the quest for global vaccine access.

Ethical Considerations in Priority Allocation: Balancing Needs and Rights

- Defining Priority Populations: This section explores the ethical considerations in prioritizing vaccine allocation, addressing questions of who should receive doses first. It delves into the balance between meeting urgent needs and respecting human rights.

- Global Standards for Fair Allocation: The narrative reflects on the development of global standards for fair vaccine allocation, emphasizing the role of ethical frameworks and international consensus in guiding distribution efforts.

Community Engagement and Education: Building Trust in Vaccination

- Importance of Community Involvement: The chapter addresses the importance of community engagement in successful vaccination campaigns. It explores strategies for building trust, fostering community involvement, and addressing concerns to ensure widespread acceptance of vaccines.

- Cultural Sensitivity in Outreach: The narrative reflects on the significance of cultural sensitivity in vaccine outreach and education, acknowledging the diverse beliefs, practices, and perceptions that influence community responses.

Post-Vaccination Challenges: Booster Shots and Variants

- Emergence of Booster Shot Debates: The section examines debates and challenges related to booster shots, exploring considerations of efficacy, equity, and global coordination in administering additional doses.

- Navigating Variants and Evolving Threats: The narrative reflects on the ongoing challenges posed by the emergence of new variants, considering the implications for vaccine distribution, public health strategies, and the need for sustained global vigilance.

By unraveling the challenges in global vaccine distribution, this chapter aims to provide readers with a comprehensive understanding of the multifaceted dilemmas faced in ensuring equitable access to COVID-19 vaccines. It sets the stage for further exploration into the societal, economic, and cultural dimensions of rebuilding and fortifying global health systems in the aftermath of the pandemic.

1. Disparities in vaccine access

In this section of "Unveiling Pain: The Global Impact of COVID-19," the narrative dives into the profound disparities in access to COVID-19 vaccines, exploring the systemic challenges that have perpetuated unequal distribution and examining efforts to bridge the global immunization divide.

Introduction to Vaccine Access Disparities

- Defining the Immunization Gulf: The chapter opens by defining the stark disparities in vaccine access that emerged during the global response to COVID-19. It explores how the distribution gap became a defining feature of the pandemic, exacerbating existing inequalities.

- Impact on Global Health Equity: The narrative emphasizes the broader implications of disparate vaccine access, ranging from persistent health disparities to economic and social ramifications for nations and communities.

Global Vaccine Inequality: The Struggle for Doses

- The Landscape of Global Vaccine Distribution: This part delves into the landscape of global vaccine distribution, highlighting the challenges faced by nations in securing an adequate supply of doses. It explores the complexities of negotiations, contracts, and geopolitical dynamics that influenced the allocation of vaccines.

- Impact on Vulnerable Populations: The narrative reflects on how global vaccine inequality disproportionately affected vulnerable populations, exacerbating health disparities and leaving marginalized communities at heightened risk.

The Role of Wealth Disparities: Securing Vaccines for Some

- Economic Influences on Access: The chapter addresses the role of wealth disparities in influencing vaccine access, examining how economic strength became a determinant in securing vaccine doses.

It explores the consequences of a system where purchasing power dictated health outcomes.

● Impacts on Low-Income Countries: The narrative reflects on the impacts of wealth-driven access on low-income countries, considering the challenges they faced in competing for and acquiring sufficient vaccine supplies.

COVAX Initiative: A Global Effort for Equity

● Overview of COVAX: This section explores the COVAX initiative, a global collaboration aimed at ensuring equitable access to COVID-19 vaccines. It delves into the goals, challenges, and achievements of COVAX in bridging the immunization gap.

● Impacts on Distribution Dynamics: The narrative reflects on the impacts of the COVAX initiative on global distribution dynamics, emphasizing its role in promoting fairness and solidarity in vaccine access.

Challenges in Supply Chain Logistics: Delivering Doses Worldwide

● Logistical Hurdles in Global Distribution: This part addresses the challenges in the global supply chain for vaccines, exploring logistical hurdles in manufacturing, transportation, and storage that hindered the equitable delivery of doses.

● Technological and Infrastructural Gaps: The narrative reflects on the technological and infrastructural gaps that played a role in impeding the efficient distribution of vaccines to all corners of the globe.

Vaccine Diplomacy and Geopolitical Implications: Power Play in Dose Distribution

● Geopolitical Influences on Vaccine Access: The chapter examines the role of vaccine diplomacy and its geopolitical implications. It explores how nations strategically used vaccine distribution as a tool for soft power and influence.

● Impacts on Global Relations: The narrative reflects on the broader impacts of vaccine diplomacy on global relations, considering both cooperative efforts and instances of competition that influenced vaccine access.

Community-Level Challenges: Education, Acceptance, and Outreach

● Importance of Community Education: This section delves into community-level challenges in vaccine access, emphasizing the importance of education, outreach, and addressing hesitancy to ensure widespread acceptance and uptake.

● Cultural Sensitivity in Vaccine Campaigns: The narrative reflects on the significance of cultural sensitivity in vaccine campaigns, acknowledging the diverse beliefs, practices, and barriers that influence community responses.

Ethical Considerations in Prioritization: Balancing Urgency and Fairness

● Defining Prioritization Criteria: This part explores the ethical considerations in prioritizing vaccine distribution, addressing questions of who should receive doses first. It delves into the balancing act between meeting urgent needs and ensuring fairness in allocation.

● Global Frameworks for Ethical Allocation: The narrative reflects on the development of global frameworks for ethical vaccine allocation, emphasizing the role of international consensus in guiding distribution efforts.

Philanthropic Interventions: Filling Gaps in Access

● Role of Philanthropy in Vaccine Access: The chapter addresses the role of philanthropic interventions in filling gaps in vaccine access. It explores initiatives from foundations, non-profits, and private sector entities that sought to contribute to global immunization efforts.

● Challenges and Opportunities: The narrative reflects on both the challenges and opportunities presented by philanthropic interventions, considering their impact on equitable vaccine distribution.

Long-Term Implications and Calls for Change

● Legacy of Vaccine Disparities: This section examines the potential long-term implications of vaccine disparities on global health, societal well-being, and economic stability. It reflects on the enduring legacy of the pandemic's unequal impact.

● Calls for Systemic Change: The narrative concludes by exploring calls for systemic change, emphasizing the need for a paradigm shift in global health governance, resource allocation, and collaborative efforts to ensure a more equitable response to future health crises.

By unraveling the disparities in vaccine access, this chapter aims to provide readers with a comprehensive understanding of the systemic challenges that contributed to unequal distribution during the COVID-19 pandemic. It sets the stage for further exploration into the societal, economic, and cultural dimensions of rebuilding and fortifying global health systems in the aftermath of this unprecedented crisis.

2. Implications for global health security

This section of "Unveiling Pain: The Global Impact of COVID-19" delves into the multifaceted implications of the pandemic for global health security. It explores the lessons learned, challenges faced, and the imperative for a renewed commitment to preparedness and collaboration in the face of future health crises.

Introduction to Global Health Security Challenges

- Defining the Post-Pandemic Landscape: The chapter opens by defining the challenges that the COVID-19 pandemic has posed to global health security. It explores the multifaceted nature of these challenges and their implications for future preparedness.

- Interconnectedness of Global Health: The narrative emphasizes the interconnectedness of global health, acknowledging that the health of one nation profoundly affects the well-being of all nations in an increasingly interdependent world.

Lessons Learned from the COVID-19 Pandemic: Building Resilience

- Reflecting on Pandemic Response: This part reflects on the lessons learned from the global response to the COVID-19 pandemic. It explores successes, failures, and the critical need for adaptability in navigating evolving health crises.

- Building Resilience: The narrative emphasizes the importance of building resilience in healthcare systems, public health infrastructure, and international cooperation to withstand and mitigate the impact of future pandemics.

Role of International Collaboration: Strengthening Alliances

- The Imperative of Global Cooperation: This section addresses the role of international collaboration in global health security. It explores how nations, organizations, and communities can strengthen alliances to foster a more coordinated and effective response to health crises.

- Frameworks for Collaborative Action: The narrative reflects on existing and potential frameworks for collaborative action, emphasizing the need for shared resources, knowledge exchange, and joint efforts to address global health threats.

Reimagining Global Health Governance: A Call for Reform

• Assessing Global Health Governance: This part examines the current state of global health governance and the need for reform. It explores the challenges in existing structures and the call for a more inclusive, agile, and responsive global health governance system.

• Opportunities for Reform: The narrative reflects on opportunities for reform in global health governance, considering how lessons from the pandemic can inform more effective structures and mechanisms for future crisis response.

Investment in Public Health Infrastructure: Fortifying Foundations

• Importance of Robust Public Health Systems: This section addresses the critical role of public health infrastructure in global health security. It explores the need for sustained investment in robust public health systems that can detect, respond to, and mitigate the impact of emerging health threats.

• Addressing Health Inequalities: The narrative reflects on how fortifying public health infrastructure contributes to addressing health inequalities, ensuring that all communities, regardless of location or socioeconomic status, have access to essential healthcare services.

Technological Advancements and Innovation: The Future of Preparedness

• Harnessing Technology for Surveillance: This part explores the role of technological advancements in enhancing global health security. It delves into how innovations in surveillance, data analytics, and communication technologies can contribute to early detection and response.

• Innovation in Vaccine Development: The narrative reflects on the innovations in vaccine development spurred by the pandemic, considering how these advancements can be leveraged for rapid response to future infectious diseases.

Capacity Building in Developing Nations: A Global Responsibility

• Addressing Disparities in Capacity: This section addresses the disparities in healthcare capacity between developed and developing nations. It explores the ethical imperative of global responsibility in building and strengthening healthcare capacity in vulnerable regions.

• Global Solidarity in Capacity Building: The narrative reflects on initiatives and frameworks for global solidarity in capacity building, emphasizing collaborative efforts to ensure that all nations are equipped to respond effectively to health crises.

The Role of Preparedness and Education: Empowering Communities

• Empowering Communities through Education: This part explores the role of preparedness and education in empowering communities to respond to health crises. It delves into the importance of public health literacy, awareness, and community engagement in building resilience.

• Crisis-Ready Communities: The narrative reflects on the vision of creating crisis-ready communities, where individuals and local entities are equipped with the knowledge and resources to contribute to a collective and coordinated response.

Climate Change and Zoonotic Threats: Addressing Root Causes

• Understanding the Link to Zoonotic Diseases: This section examines the link between climate change, environmental degradation, and the emergence of zoonotic diseases. It explores the need to address root causes and promote sustainable practices to prevent future pandemics.

● Interdisciplinary Approaches: The narrative reflects on the importance of interdisciplinary approaches that consider the interconnectedness of human, animal, and environmental health in addressing the root causes of zoonotic threats.

Global Commitment to One Health: Integrating Human, Animal, and Environmental Health

● One Health as a Framework: This chapter concludes by exploring the concept of One Health as a holistic framework for global health security. It emphasizes the integration of human, animal, and environmental health, recognizing their interdependence in preventing and mitigating the impact of pandemics.

● A Shared Responsibility: The narrative reflects on the idea that global health security is a shared responsibility, requiring collaboration, innovation, and sustained commitment from individuals, communities, nations, and international organizations.

By examining the implications for global health security, this chapter aims to provide readers with insights into the transformative changes needed to navigate a new era of preparedness and collaboration. It sets the stage for further exploration into the societal, economic, and cultural dimensions of rebuilding and fortifying global health systems in the aftermath of the COVID-19 pandemic.

VII. Social and Cultural Disruption

In this section of "Unveiling Pain: The Global Impact of COVID-19," we explore the profound social and cultural disruptions brought about by the pandemic. From the reshaping of daily life to the reevaluation of societal norms, the narratives within this chapter illuminate the ways in which COVID-19 has not only affected physical health but has also woven its impact into the intricate threads of human society and culture.

Introduction to Social and Cultural Disruption

- Defining the New Normal: The chapter begins by defining the concept of the "new normal" that emerged in the wake of the pandemic. It explores how COVID-19 disrupted the familiar patterns of human interaction, societal structures, and cultural practices.

- Impact on Social Fabric: The narrative emphasizes the far-reaching impact of social and cultural disruption, acknowledging that the repercussions extend beyond the immediate health crisis and shape the way societies function.

Transformations in Daily Life: Rethinking Routine

- Altered Daily Practices: This section delves into the transformations in daily life brought about by the pandemic. It explores how lockdowns, remote work, and changes in mobility patterns have reshaped the routines and habits of individuals and families worldwide.

- Challenges and Opportunities: The narrative reflects on the challenges and opportunities presented by these changes, considering both the difficulties in adjusting to new norms and the potential for positive shifts in work-life balance and environmental impact.

Impact on Human Connection: Navigating Isolation and Distancing
Loneliness and Isolation: This part explores the impact of social distancing measures on human connection. It delves into the experiences of loneliness and isolation, examining the emotional toll of being physically separated from loved ones and communities.

- Creative Solutions for Connection: The narrative reflects on the creative solutions individuals and communities devised to maintain connection—from virtual gatherings to innovative ways of supporting one another during times of isolation.

Changes in Cultural Celebrations and Traditions

- Altered Festivities: This section addresses the disruptions to cultural celebrations and traditions caused by the pandemic. It explores how holidays, ceremonies, and cultural events were transformed, emphasizing the resilience of communities in adapting to new ways of commemorating important occasions.

- Preserving Cultural Heritage: The narrative reflects on efforts to preserve cultural heritage and traditions amidst the challenges posed by restrictions, considering the role of innovation and adaptation in sustaining cultural practices.

Economic Disparities and Social Inequities

- Exacerbation of Inequalities: This part examines the widening economic disparities and social inequities brought to light by the pandemic. It explores how vulnerable populations were disproportionately affected, facing heightened challenges in areas such as healthcare access, education, and employment.

- Calls for Social Justice: The narrative reflects on the calls for social justice that intensified during the pandemic, emphasizing the need for systemic changes to address long standing inequalities and promote a more just and equitable society.

Challenges to Education: Remote Learning and the Digital Divide

- Disruption in Educational Systems: This section addresses the challenges to education posed by the shift to remote learning. It explores the impact of the digital divide on students and educators, highlighting disparities in access to online education.

- Innovations in Education: The narrative reflects on innovations in education that emerged in response to the disruptions, considering the potential for technology to democratize learning and bridge educational gaps.

Shifts in Work Culture: Remote Work and the Future of Employment

- Remote Work Dynamics: This part delves into the shifts in work culture brought about by the widespread adoption of remote work. It explores the challenges and benefits of this new work paradigm and its potential long-term implications for the future of employment.

- Reimagining Work-Life Balance: The narrative reflects on the reimagining of work-life balance, considering how the pandemic prompted a reassessment of traditional workplace structures and expectations.

Crisis as Catalyst for Social Innovation

- Innovative Responses to Crisis: This section explores how the crisis acted as a catalyst for social innovation. It highlights stories of communities, organizations, and individuals coming together to address emerging challenges and create solutions in the face of adversity.

● Sustainable and Inclusive Practices: The narrative reflects on the potential for sustainable and inclusive practices to emerge from the crucible of crisis, emphasizing the importance of collective action and creativity in navigating uncertain times.

Mental Health and Well-Being: Addressing the Silent Pandemic

● Rising Mental Health Challenges: This part examines the rising mental health challenges exacerbated by the pandemic. It explores the impact of stress, anxiety, and grief on individuals and communities, acknowledging mental health as a silent pandemic that demands attention.

● Destigmatizing Mental Health: The narrative reflects on the importance of destigmatizing mental health issues, fostering open conversations, and promoting supportive environments to address the psychological toll of the pandemic.

Cultural Resilience and Hope

● The Resilience of Cultural Expression: This chapter concludes by highlighting stories of cultural resilience and hope. It explores how communities found strength in cultural expression, creativity, and shared narratives, emphasizing the role of culture in fostering resilience during challenging times.

● Building a Hopeful Future: The narrative reflects on the potential for building a hopeful future, grounded in the resilience of human connection, cultural identity, and the shared experiences that transcend the disruptions of the pandemic.

By exploring the social and cultural disruptions caused by COVID-19, this chapter aims to provide readers with a nuanced understanding of the profound changes that have reshaped the fabric of normalcy. It sets the stage for further exploration into the societal, economic, and health dimensions of rebuilding and fortifying global systems in the aftermath of this transformative event.

A. Changes in societal norms and behaviors

This section of "Unveiling Pain: The Global Impact of COVID-19" delves into the significant shifts in societal norms and behaviors brought about by the pandemic. It explores the transformative impact on the way individuals interact, communities function, and societies evolve in response to the unprecedented challenges posed by COVID-19.

Introduction to Societal Norms in Flux

- Defining the Evolution: The chapter begins by defining the dynamic evolution of societal norms in the wake of the pandemic. It explores the profound changes that have shaped human behavior, interaction, and collective consciousness.

- Impact on Cultural Identity: The narrative underscores how these shifts extend beyond individual behaviors, influencing cultural identity and the shared values that define communities.

Adaptations to Social Distancing: Balancing Connection and Safety

- Redefining Personal Space: This part examines the adaptations individuals have made to the concept of personal space and social distancing. It explores the challenges and innovations in maintaining connections while prioritizing safety.

- Impacts on Social Rituals: The narrative reflects on how social rituals, from greetings to communal events, have been reshaped to align with the imperative of social distancing and the preservation of public health.

Remote Work and the Redefinition of Professional Interaction

- The Rise of Remote Work: This section explores the widespread adoption of remote work and its impact on professional interaction.

It delves into the challenges and benefits of virtual workspaces, examining how this shift has redefined traditional notions of professional engagement.

• Balancing Productivity and Well-Being: The narrative reflects on the balancing act between productivity and well-being in the remote work paradigm, considering the potential long-term implications for the future of employment.

Reshaping Education: Blended Learning and Technological Integration

• Blended Learning Models: This part addresses the reshaping of education through blended learning models and increased technological integration. It explores how educational institutions adapted to remote and hybrid learning environments to ensure continuity in the face of disruptions.

• Equity in Educational Access: The narrative reflects on the challenges and opportunities presented by these changes, considering how technological advancements can be leveraged to address educational disparities and promote inclusive learning.

Health and Hygiene Practices: The New Imperatives

• Elevated Awareness of Health Practices: This section examines the heightened awareness of health and hygiene practices. It explores how individuals and communities have embraced new norms related to hand hygiene, mask-wearing, and other preventive measures.

• Cultural Shifts in Health Consciousness: The narrative reflects on the cultural shifts in health consciousness, emphasizing the potential for sustained adherence to preventive measures and the impact on public health beyond the pandemic.

Community Support and Mutual Aid: Reinventing Solidarity

- Rise of Community Support Networks: This part delves into the rise of community support networks and mutual aid initiatives. It explores how individuals and organizations came together to provide assistance, resources, and emotional support during times of crisis.

- Reinventing Solidarity: The narrative reflects on the reinvention of solidarity within communities, considering the lasting impact of collective efforts to address shared challenges.

Digital Transformation: Accelerating Connectivity

- Acceleration of Digitalization: This section addresses the acceleration of digital transformation in various aspects of life. It explores how the pandemic acted as a catalyst for the adoption of digital technologies, influencing communication, commerce, and social interaction.

- Challenges and Opportunities: The narrative reflects on the challenges and opportunities presented by the rapid digitization of society, considering both the potential benefits and risks associated with increased reliance on technology.

Shifts in Consumer Behavior: From Necessities to Priorities:

- Reevaluation of Consumer Priorities: This part examines the reevaluation of consumer priorities and spending habits. It explores how individuals reassessed what is essential and non-essential, leading to shifts in consumption patterns and economic behavior.

- Impact on Business Models: The narrative reflects on the impact of changing consumer behavior on business models, considering how industries adapted to meet evolving demands and expectations.

Cultural Reckoning: Addressing Inequities and Social Justice

● Heightened Awareness of Injustices: This section addresses the cultural reckoning sparked by the pandemic, particularly in addressing systemic inequities and issues of social justice. It explores how movements gained momentum, advocating for change on local and global scales.

● Calls for Structural Reform: The narrative reflects on the calls for structural reform, considering the potential for lasting change in societal norms and policies that promote inclusivity, diversity, and equity.

Psychological Resilience and Coping Mechanisms

● Building Psychological Resilience: This chapter concludes by highlighting stories of psychological resilience and coping mechanisms. It explores how individuals and communities developed strategies to navigate uncertainty, anxiety, and grief, emphasizing the importance of mental well-being in adapting to a changed world.

● Lessons in Adaptability: The narrative reflects on the lessons learned in adaptability, emphasizing the capacity of human societies to evolve, reimagine, and find strength in the face of unprecedented challenges.

By examining changes in societal norms and behaviors, this chapter aims to provide readers with insights into the transformative nature of the pandemic on human interaction, community dynamics, and cultural identity. It sets the stage for further exploration into the societal, economic, and health dimensions of rebuilding and fortifying global systems in the aftermath of this transformative event.

1. Impact on social interactions

This section of "Unveiling Pain: The Global Impact of COVID-19" explores the profound impact of the pandemic on social interactions, unraveling how the fabric of human connection has been reshaped in the era of social distancing and public health imperatives.

Introduction to the Altered Landscape of Social Interaction

- Defining the Social Paradigm Shift: The chapter begins by defining the altered landscape of social interaction brought about by the pandemic. It explores the seismic shifts in how people connect, communicate, and engage with one another.

- The Dual Nature of Impact: The narrative underscores the dual nature of the impact, acknowledging the challenges of physical separation while also recognizing the emergence of innovative ways to foster connection.

Social Distancing and Its Emotional Toll

- Challenges of Physical Separation: This part delves into the challenges posed by social distancing, exploring the emotional toll of physical separation from loved ones, friends, and broader social circles.

- Nurturing Emotional Well-Being: The narrative reflects on strategies individuals employed to nurture emotional well-being, emphasizing the importance of maintaining a sense of connection despite the constraints of physical distance.

Virtual Communication: The Rise of Digital Connectivity

- Acceleration of Virtual Platforms: This section addresses the acceleration of virtual communication platforms as a primary means of staying connected. It explores how video calls, messaging apps, and social media became lifelines for maintaining relationships.

- Reimagining Social Gatherings Online: The narrative reflects on the reimagining of social gatherings in the digital realm, considering both the challenges and opportunities presented by virtual connectivity.

Shifts in Friendships and Social Circles

● Dynamic Changes in Social Dynamics: This part examines the dynamic changes in friendships and social circles. It explores how the pandemic prompted reevaluations of social priorities, leading to shifts in the composition and dynamics of social networks.

● The Evolution of Social Support Systems: The narrative reflects on the evolution of social support systems, considering how individuals navigated changes in their social circles to adapt to the new normal.

Community Resilience: Mutual Aid and Support Networks

● Rise of Community Support: This section explores the rise of community support networks and mutual aid initiatives. It delves into how neighborhoods, local organizations, and online communities came together to provide assistance, resources, and emotional support.

● Fostering Resilient Communities: The narrative reflects on the resilience of communities in supporting one another, emphasizing the potential for lasting positive impacts on local social fabrics.

Challenges in Romantic Relationships: Navigating Uncertainty

● Impact on Romantic Partnerships: This part addresses the challenges faced by romantic relationships. It explores how couples navigated uncertainties, physical separations, and the strain on relational dynamics during lockdowns and social restrictions.

● Adaptations and Innovations: The narrative reflects on the adaptations and innovations in maintaining romantic connections, considering the ways in which couples found resilience and strength in the face of adversity.

Generational Perspectives: Impact on Children, Teens, and the Elderly

● Educational and Social Challenges for Youth: This section examines the impact on different age groups, including children, teens, and the elderly. It explores the educational and social challenges faced by youth, as well as the unique considerations for the elderly population.

• Intergenerational Connection: The narrative reflects on efforts to bridge generational gaps, considering initiatives that fostered connection and understanding between different age groups.

The Role of Rituals and Celebrations: Redefining Commemoration

• Transformation of Cultural and Personal Rituals: This part delves into the transformation of cultural and personal rituals. It explores how celebrations, ceremonies, and communal traditions were redefined, emphasizing the creative ways individuals and communities found to commemorate important milestones.

• Cultural Adaptations: The narrative reflects on the cultural adaptations that emerged, considering the resilience of human creativity in maintaining a sense of connection during times of physical separation.

Impact on Social Anxiety and Mental Health

• Exacerbation of Social Anxiety: This section addresses the exacerbation of social anxiety and mental health challenges. It explores the impact of prolonged social isolation on individuals' mental well-being and the strategies employed to navigate these difficulties.

• Destigmatizing Mental Health Conversations: The narrative reflects on the importance of destigmatizing mental health conversations, emphasizing the need for open dialogue and support systems to address the psychological impact of disrupted social interactions.

Lessons Learned and Future Outlook

● Adapting to a Changed Social Landscape: This chapter concludes by highlighting lessons learned from the transformed landscape of social interactions. It reflects on how individuals and societies adapted to a changed social landscape and considers the future outlook for human connection in a post-pandemic world.

● Resilience and Innovation: The narrative emphasizes the resilience and innovation displayed in navigating the challenges of altered social interactions, setting the stage for continued exploration of societal, economic, and health dimensions in the aftermath of the global pandemic.

By exploring the impact on social interactions, this chapter aims to provide readers with a nuanced understanding of the ways in which human connection has evolved and adapted in response to the challenges posed by COVID-19. It sets the stage for further exploration into the broader societal implications and the collective journey toward a transformed future.

2. Shifts in cultural practices

In this section of "Unveiling Pain: The Global Impact of COVID-19," we delve into the transformative shifts in cultural practices, exploring how communities worldwide have adapted their traditions, ceremonies, and rituals in response to the challenges posed by the pandemic.

Introduction to Cultural Transformation

● Defining Cultural Adaptation: The chapter begins by defining the cultural transformation spurred by the pandemic. It explores the dynamic ways in which societies have adapted their cultural practices to navigate the complexities of the global health crisis.

● The Resilience of Culture: The narrative underscores the resilience of culture, acknowledging its ability to evolve and endure even in the face of unprecedented challenges.

Transformations in Communal Celebrations: Rethinking Festivals and Events

• Impact on Festivals and Events: This part examines the impact of the pandemic on communal celebrations, festivals, and events. It explores how restrictions on gatherings prompted communities to rethink and adapt traditional festivities.

• Virtual and Hybrid Celebrations: The narrative reflects on the emergence of virtual and hybrid celebrations, considering the ways in which technology was employed to maintain cultural connections while adhering to safety measures.

Religious Practices in the Digital Age

• Shifts in Religious Observances: This section addresses the shifts in religious practices brought about by the pandemic. It explores how religious communities adapted their rituals, worship services, and pilgrimages to accommodate health and safety guidelines.

• Digital Worship Platforms: The narrative reflects on the rise of digital worship platforms and virtual religious gatherings, considering their impact on the accessibility and inclusivity of religious practices.

Changes in Cultural Rituals: Navigating Life's Milestones

• Redefining Life's Milestones: This part delves into the changes in cultural rituals associated with life's milestones, including births, weddings, and funerals. It explores how communities navigated the challenges of commemorating these significant events while adhering to safety measures.

• Innovations in Ceremony: The narrative reflects on the innovations in ceremony and ritual, considering how communities found creative ways to honor traditions in the context of the pandemic.

Cultural Heritage Preservation: Museums, Arts, and Preservation Efforts

- Impact on Museums and Arts: This section examines the impact of the pandemic on cultural institutions, including museums, galleries, and performing arts. It explores how these entities adapted to closures and restrictions, as well as the innovations in digital platforms to showcase cultural heritage.

- Preservation Efforts: The narrative reflects on preservation efforts, considering the importance of safeguarding cultural heritage during times of crisis and the role of technology in fostering global access to cultural artifacts.

LANGUAGE AND COMMUNICATION: Evolution in Expression

- Changes in Language Use: This part addresses the evolution in language use and communication. It explores how linguistic expressions adapted to reflect the new normal, introducing terms and phrases that captured the unique challenges and experiences of the pandemic.

- Digital Communication Dynamics: The narrative reflects on the dynamics of digital communication, considering the impact of technology on language evolution and the ways in which virtual interactions shaped cultural expression.

Culinary Transformations: Home Cooking and Cultural Identity

- Return to Home Cooking: This section examines culinary transformations during the pandemic. It explores the resurgence of home cooking, as individuals and families rediscovered traditional recipes and culinary practices as a source of comfort and connection.

• Cultural Identity Through Food: The narrative reflects on the connection between culinary practices and cultural identity, considering how food became a powerful means of maintaining cultural ties and traditions.

Arts and Creativity in Quarantine: Expressions of Resilience

• Resilience in Artistic Expression: This part delves into the arts and creativity that emerged during quarantine. It explores how individuals and communities turned to artistic expression as a means of resilience, capturing the collective experiences and emotions of the pandemic.

• Digital Platforms for Artistic Showcase: The narrative reflects on the role of digital platforms in showcasing and preserving artistic expressions, considering the potential for a more democratized and globally accessible art landscape.

Indigenous Perspectives: Balancing Tradition and Public Health

• Challenges for Indigenous Communities: This section addresses the unique challenges faced by indigenous communities. It explores how these communities balanced the preservation of cultural practices with the imperative of safeguarding public health.

• Innovations in Cultural Conservation: The narrative reflects on the innovations in cultural conservation within indigenous communities, considering how traditional knowledge and practices were adapted for resilience.

Globalization and Local Adaptations: Cultural Hybridity in a Changing World

• Globalization's Impact: This chapter concludes by examining the impact of globalization on cultural practices. It reflects on how local traditions adapted to global influences and how the interconnected world navigated a collective cultural response to the pandemic.

● Cultural Hybridity: The narrative emphasizes the concept of cultural hybridity, exploring the ways in which diverse cultural practices intermingle, evolve, and contribute to the rich tapestry of a changing global cultural landscape.

By exploring shifts in cultural practices, this chapter aims to provide readers with a nuanced understanding of the adaptive resilience of cultural identity in the face of unprecedented challenges. It sets the stage for further exploration into the broader societal implications and the collective journey toward a transformed and interconnected future.

VIII. Hope and Resilience

In this section of "Unveiling Pain: The Global Impact of COVID-19," we explore the profound themes of hope and resilience that have emerged in response to the challenges presented by the pandemic. This chapter aims to inspire and uplift, highlighting the stories of individuals, communities, and nations that have demonstrated remarkable strength in the face of adversity.

Introduction to Hope Amidst Desolation

- Defining Hope and Resilience: The chapter begins by defining the transformative concepts of hope and resilience in the context of the global impact of COVID-19. It explores the psychological, social, and cultural dimensions of these themes.

- The Human Spirit's Capacity: The narrative underscores the extraordinary capacity of the human spirit to find hope and resilience, even in the midst of profound pain and uncertainty.

Individual Stories of Triumph: Overcoming Personal Challenges

- Personal Narratives of Triumph: This part delves into individual stories of triumph, showcasing the resilience of people who faced personal challenges during the pandemic. It explores tales of recovery, adaptation, and personal growth in the midst of adversity.

- Lessons from Adversity: The narrative reflects on the lessons drawn from personal challenges, considering how individuals discovered newfound strength and purpose through their journeys.

Community Bonds and Solidarity: Stories of Collective Strength

● Community Solidarity: This section explores stories of community bonds and solidarity. It delves into the ways in which communities came together to support one another, emphasizing the power of collective strength in navigating shared challenges.

● Innovative Community Solutions: The narrative reflects on the innovative solutions and support networks that emerged within communities, fostering a sense of shared purpose and resilience.

NATIONAL RESPONSES: Governments and Societal Resilience

● Governmental and Societal Resilience: This part examines the responses of governments and societies on a national level. It explores instances where nations rallied together, implemented effective policies, and demonstrated resilience in the face of healthcare, economic, and social challenges.

● Global Cooperation: The narrative reflects on examples of global cooperation, acknowledging instances where nations collaborated to share resources, knowledge, and support in the fight against the pandemic.

Scientific Breakthroughs and Medical Advances

● Milestones in Medical Research: This section highlights scientific breakthroughs and medical advances that offered hope in the battle against the virus. It explores the rapid development of vaccines, innovative treatment methods, and the tireless efforts of healthcare professionals on the frontlines.

● The Promise of Future Preparedness: The narrative reflects on the promise these advancements hold for future global health crises, emphasizing the importance of continued investment in scientific research and healthcare infrastructure.

Educational Innovations: Nurturing a Resilient Future Generation

• Adaptations in Education: This part delves into educational innovations that emerged in response to school closures and the shift to remote learning. It explores how educators, students, and parents adapted to new methods of teaching and learning, emphasizing the resilience of the education system.

• Empowering the Next Generation: The narrative reflects on the empowerment of the next generation through these educational adaptations, considering the potential for a more resilient and adaptable workforce.

Economic Recovery Stories: Rebuilding Livelihoods

• Recovery of Businesses and Livelihoods: This section examines stories of economic recovery and rebuilding livelihoods. It explores how businesses adapted, individuals pivoted careers, and communities found innovative solutions to address the economic fallout of the pandemic.

• Entrepreneurial Resilience: The narrative reflects on the entrepreneurial resilience demonstrated by individuals who turned adversity into opportunity, showcasing the capacity for innovation and adaptability in the face of economic challenges.

Cultural Expressions of Hope: Art, Music, and Creativity

• Artistic Responses to Adversity: This part explores cultural expressions of hope through art, music, and creativity. It examines how artists and creators used their talents to inspire, uplift, and provide solace during challenging times.

• Cultural Healing: The narrative reflects on the healing power of cultural expressions, considering the ways in which art and creativity served as a source of comfort and connection for individuals and communities.

Global Environmental Resilience: Nature's Recovery and Conservation Efforts

● Nature's Recovery: This section delves into global environmental resilience, highlighting positive impacts on nature and conservation efforts during lockdowns and reduced human activity. It explores how ecosystems showed signs of recovery, emphasizing the interconnectedness of human well-being and environmental health.

● Sustainable Practices: The narrative reflects on the lessons learned about sustainable practices and the potential for a more harmonious relationship between humanity and the environment.

Lessons for the Future: Building a Resilient Tomorrow

● Reflections on Collective Learning: This chapter concludes by reflecting on the lessons learned and the path forward. It explores how the experiences of hope and resilience during the pandemic can inform future preparedness, collaboration, and global solidarity.

● Building a Resilient Tomorrow: The narrative emphasizes the importance of building a resilient future, grounded in the lessons of the past, and encourages readers to carry the spirit of hope and resilience forward in the collective journey toward recovery and renewal.

By exploring stories of hope and resilience, this chapter aims to inspire readers and instill a sense of optimism for the future. It sets the stage for further exploration into the societal, economic, and health dimensions of rebuilding and fortifying global systems in the aftermath of this transformative event.

A. Stories of communities coming together

In this section of "Unveiling Pain: The Global Impact of COVID-19," we explore poignant stories of communities coming together, weaving a tapestry of resilience and solidarity in the face of unprecedented challenges.

Introduction to Collective Resilience

- Defining Collective Resilience: The chapter begins by defining the concept of collective resilience and the power of communities to unite in the face of adversity. It explores the transformative impact of shared strength and mutual support.

- The Thread of Unity: The narrative underscores the thread of unity that binds communities, emphasizing how this unity becomes a powerful force during times of crisis.

Local Initiatives: Community-Led Responses to Crisis

- Grassroots Initiatives: This part delves into grassroots initiatives that emerged within communities. It explores how local leaders, organizations, and individuals took the initiative to address pressing needs, from healthcare support to ensuring access to essential resources.

- Stories of Local Heroes: The narrative reflects on the stories of local heroes—individuals whose actions made a significant impact on the well-being of their communities during challenging times.

Support Networks for Vulnerable Populations: Nurturing Inclusivity

- Assistance for Vulnerable Groups: This section examines the formation of support networks catering to vulnerable populations. It explores how communities rallied to provide assistance, resources, and emotional support to those disproportionately affected by the pandemic, including the elderly, low-income families, and marginalized groups.

● Fostering Inclusivity: The narrative reflects on the importance of fostering inclusivity within community support networks, ensuring that no one is left behind in the collective journey towards recovery.

Neighborhood Solidarity: Acts of Kindness Close to Home

● Acts of Kindness: This part explores acts of kindness and solidarity within neighborhoods. It delves into stories of individuals supporting one another, whether through grocery shopping for neighbors, organizing neighborhood check-ins, or creating initiatives to foster a sense of community spirit.

● Building Stronger Local Bonds: The narrative reflects on the role of these acts of kindness in building stronger local bonds, emphasizing the significance of community cohesion in times of crisis.

Digital Communities: Connectivity Beyond Borders

● Online Support Networks: This section addresses the role of digital communities in fostering connectivity beyond physical borders. It explores how online platforms became spaces for mutual support, information sharing, and virtual gatherings, transcending geographical limitations.

● Global Perspectives: The narrative reflects on the global perspectives that emerged within digital communities, highlighting the interconnectedness of people from diverse backgrounds who came together to navigate the challenges of the pandemic.

Community-Led Healthcare Initiatives: Supporting Frontline Workers

● Community Support for Healthcare Workers: This part examines community-led initiatives to support healthcare workers on the frontlines. It explores how individuals and organizations mobilized resources, provided meals, and offered emotional support to those tirelessly working to combat the virus.

● Acknowledging Frontline Sacrifices: The narrative reflects on the acknowledgment of frontline sacrifices, emphasizing the importance of recognizing and supporting healthcare workers as integral members of the community.

Educational Collaborations: Nurturing Learning Environments

● Collaborations in Education: This section explores collaborations within communities to nurture learning environments. It examines how parents, educators, and local organizations worked together to support students during the challenges of remote learning and educational disruptions.

● Innovative Educational Solutions: The narrative reflects on innovative educational solutions that emerged at the community level, considering how adaptability and collaboration became essential components of sustaining learning environments.

Cultural Preservation Projects: Safeguarding Heritage and Traditions

● Community-Led Cultural Preservation: This part delves into community-led projects focused on cultural preservation. It explores how communities engaged in initiatives to safeguard cultural heritage, traditions, and local practices amidst the disruptions caused by the pandemic.

● Promoting Cultural Resilience: The narrative reflects on the promotion of cultural resilience within communities, emphasizing the role of these projects in maintaining a sense of identity and continuity.

Environmental Stewardship: Local Efforts for Global Impact

● Local Environmental Initiatives: This section addresses local efforts for global environmental impact. It explores how communities engaged in environmental stewardship projects, from neighborhood clean-ups to sustainable practices, contributing to a collective movement towards a healthier planet.

● Global Connectivity Through Environmental Action: The narrative reflects on the interconnectedness of global environmental issues and the impact of localized efforts on the broader ecosystem.

BUILDING LONG-TERM Community Resilience: Lessons for the Future

● Reflections on Long-Term Resilience: This chapter concludes by reflecting on the lessons learned from community resilience during the pandemic. It explores how these stories can inform long-term strategies for community well-being, preparedness, and resilience in the face of future challenges.

● Building a Resilient Future: The narrative emphasizes the importance of building a resilient future grounded in the lessons of collective strength and unity. It sets the stage for continued exploration into the societal, economic, and health dimensions of rebuilding and fortifying global systems in the aftermath of this transformative event.

By delving into stories of communities coming together, this chapter aims to inspire readers and showcase the indomitable spirit of human connection and support that emerged during a time of shared adversity. It serves as a testament to the resilience inherent in communities and highlights the potential for positive, community-driven change in the face of global challenges.

1. Acts of kindness and solidarity

In this segment of "Unveiling Pain: The Global Impact of COVID-19," we explore heartwarming stories of acts of kindness and solidarity that emerged from the darkness of the pandemic, illustrating the resilience and compassion embedded in the human spirit.

Introduction to Acts of Compassion

- Defining Acts of Kindness: The chapter begins by defining acts of kindness as moments of compassion, empathy, and support that individuals extended to one another during the pandemic. It explores the transformative impact of these gestures on both the giver and the receiver.

- The Ripple Effect: The narrative underscores the ripple effect of acts of kindness, illustrating how small, compassionate actions can reverberate through communities and contribute to a collective sense of hope.

Neighborhood Heroes: Supporting Each Other Close to Home

- Grocery Runs and Errand Assistance: This part delves into stories of neighbors stepping up to support one another. It explores instances where individuals offered to run errands, pick up groceries, and provide essential supplies for those who were unable to leave their homes.

- Creating a Supportive Microcosm: The narrative reflects on the creation of supportive microcosms within neighborhoods, emphasizing the impact of these small-scale acts on fostering a sense of community.

Community Gardens and Food Sharing Initiatives

- Local Food Initiatives: This section explores community-led efforts to address food insecurity. It examines the establishment of community gardens, food banks, and sharing initiatives where surplus produce and meals were distributed to those in need.

● Nourishing Both Body and Soul: The narrative reflects on the dual impact of these initiatives, providing not only nourishment for the body but also a sense of communal care and solidarity.

Mask-Making Campaigns: Crafting Protection and Connection

● Handmade Masks for All: This part highlights grassroots movements where individuals and groups engaged in making and distributing masks. It explores how the act of creating protective gear became a symbol of care and responsibility within communities.

● Fostering a Sense of Connection: The narrative reflects on the symbolism of handmade masks, emphasizing the connection forged through shared efforts to protect one another.

Volunteerism in Healthcare Support: Extending a Helping Hand to Frontline Workers

● Volunteer Support for Healthcare Workers: This section explores stories of individuals volunteering their time and skills to support healthcare workers. It delves into initiatives such as providing meals, offering emotional support, and assisting with non-medical tasks to alleviate the burden on those on the frontlines.

● Recognizing the Human Faces Behind Healthcare: The narrative reflects on the importance of recognizing the human faces behind healthcare, emphasizing the gratitude expressed through volunteer efforts.

Global PPE Drives: Collaborative Efforts for Protection

● International PPE Drives: This part examines international efforts to provide personal protective equipment (PPE) to regions facing shortages. It explores collaborations between countries, organizations, and individuals to ensure that healthcare professionals had the resources they needed to stay safe.

- Solidarity Across Borders: The narrative reflects on the global solidarity exhibited through PPE drives, illustrating the interconnectedness of the world in the face of a shared health crisis.

Tech-Savvy Generosity: Bridging the Digital Divide

- Digital Device Donations: This section delves into initiatives addressing the digital divide exacerbated by remote work and learning. It explores the donation of devices, such as laptops and tablets, to ensure that individuals, especially students, had the necessary tools for virtual communication and education.

- Empowering Through Connectivity: The narrative reflects on the empowerment facilitated by digital device donations, emphasizing the role of technology in maintaining connectivity and access to education.

Elderly Care Packages: Nurturing the Most Vulnerable

- Care Packages for the Elderly: This part explores initiatives focused on providing care packages to the elderly. It examines how communities came together to create packages containing essentials, entertainment, and heartfelt notes to combat the isolation experienced by older individuals.

- Addressing Loneliness Through Compassion: The narrative reflects on the emotional impact of care packages, addressing not only physical needs but also combating the loneliness experienced by the elderly during lockdowns.

Educational Mentorship Programs: Supporting Students Virtually

- Virtual Mentorship Initiatives: This section highlights mentorship programs that emerged to support students facing challenges in remote learning. It explores how individuals volunteered their time to provide academic support, mentorship, and encouragement to students navigating virtual education.

● Fostering a Sense of Academic Community: The narrative reflects on the creation of virtual academic communities, emphasizing the importance of supportive relationships in the educational journey.

Letters of Hope: Penning Encouragement Across Distances

● Letter-Writing Campaigns: This chapter concludes by exploring campaigns centered around handwritten letters of hope. It delves into initiatives where individuals, especially those in isolation, received letters of encouragement, inspiration, and solidarity from strangers around the world.

● The Power of Written Connection: The narrative reflects on the profound power of written connection, emphasizing the emotional impact of receiving heartfelt letters during times of physical separation.

By illuminating these stories of acts of kindness and solidarity, this chapter aims to showcase the innate compassion within communities and the transformative effect of these actions on both individuals and the collective. It sets the stage for continued exploration into the broader societal, economic, and health dimensions of rebuilding and fortifying global systems in the aftermath of this transformative event.

2. Innovations and adaptations in response to challenges

In this segment of "Unveiling Pain: The Global Impact of COVID-19," we explore the innovative and adaptive responses that emerged globally in the face of unprecedented challenges, showcasing the remarkable resilience of individuals, communities, and organizations.

Introduction to Adaptive Responses

● Defining Innovation and Adaptation: The chapter begins by defining innovation and adaptation as the creative responses that individuals and communities devised to address challenges presented by the pandemic. It explores the transformative impact of these responses on redefining societal norms and structures.

• The Power of Human Ingenuity: The narrative underscores the power of human ingenuity, emphasizing how the collective response to adversity sparked inventive solutions and new ways of approaching longstanding issues.

TELEMEDICINE REVOLUTION: Healthcare at a Distance

• Rise of Telemedicine Platforms: This part delves into the rapid adoption of telemedicine as a response to healthcare challenges. It explores how healthcare providers and patients embraced virtual consultations, remote monitoring, and telehealth platforms to ensure continued access to medical services while minimizing the risk of viral transmission.

• Democratizing Healthcare Access: The narrative reflects on the democratization of healthcare access through telemedicine, highlighting how technology bridged gaps and provided medical support to individuals regardless of geographical constraints.

Remote Work and Digital Transformation: Shaping the Future of Work

• Acceleration of Remote Work: This section explores the acceleration of remote work and digital transformation across industries. It examines how organizations adapted to the challenges of lockdowns and social distancing by implementing remote work policies, virtual collaboration tools, and digital platforms.

• Redefined Work-Life Dynamics: The narrative reflects on the redefined work-life dynamics, emphasizing the potential long-term impacts on workplace culture, flexibility, and the use of technology in shaping the future of work.

Distance Learning Evolution: Navigating Educational Disruptions

● Shift to Online Education: This part delves into the shift to online education as a response to the closure of schools and universities. It explores how educators, students, and educational institutions adapted to virtual classrooms, e-learning platforms, and innovative teaching methods.

● Empowering Lifelong Learners: The narrative reflects on the empowerment of lifelong learners through online education, considering the potential for increased accessibility and inclusivity in the educational landscape.

Contactless Solutions: Redefining Consumer Interactions

● Contactless Payments and Services: This section examines the widespread adoption of contactless solutions in various industries. It explores how businesses and consumers embraced contactless payments, delivery services, and touchless technologies to reduce physical contact and minimize the risk of viral transmission.

● Reshaping Consumer Expectations: The narrative reflects on the reshaping of consumer expectations, emphasizing the importance of convenience, safety, and efficiency in contactless solutions.

Community-Led Food Initiatives: Sustainable Agriculture and Local Markets

● Rise of Community Gardens: This part highlights the rise of community gardens and sustainable agriculture initiatives. It explores how communities embraced local food production, farmers' markets, and sustainable practices to address disruptions in the global food supply chain.

• Building Food Resilience: The narrative reflects on the building of food resilience at the community level, emphasizing the importance of local initiatives in ensuring access to fresh and sustainable produce.

Economic Innovations: Small Business Adaptations and Digital Entrepreneurship

• Adaptations by Small Businesses: This section delves into the adaptations made by small businesses to navigate economic challenges. It explores how entrepreneurs embraced digital platforms, e-commerce, and innovative business models to sustain and grow their enterprises.

• The Rise of Digital Entrepreneurship: The narrative reflects on the rise of digital entrepreneurship, highlighting how individuals turned challenges into opportunities through creativity and adaptability.

Smart Cities and Urban Planning: Redesigning Public Spaces

• Urban Planning for Social Distancing: This part explores innovations in urban planning to accommodate social distancing measures. It examines how cities reimagined public spaces, transportation systems, and infrastructure to prioritize safety and well-being.

• Towards Sustainable and Resilient Cities: The narrative reflects on the potential for sustainable and resilient urban development, emphasizing the importance of adaptable city planning in the face of global challenges.

Virtual Cultural Experiences: Arts and Entertainment in the Digital Realm

• Digital Arts and Performances: This section highlights the digital transformation of the arts and entertainment industry. It explores how artists, performers, and cultural institutions adapted to virtual platforms, bringing cultural experiences to audiences worldwide despite physical limitations.

● Global Accessibility to Cultural Offerings: The narrative reflects on the global accessibility of cultural offerings, considering how virtual experiences expanded audience reach and participation in the arts.

Environmental Conservation Through Behavioral Changes

● Reduction in Carbon Emissions: This chapter concludes by exploring the unintended positive consequences of behavioral changes during lockdowns. It examines how reduced human activity led to temporary improvements in air quality, reduced carbon emissions, and positive impacts on the environment.

● Lessons for Sustainable Living: The narrative reflects on the lessons learned for sustainable living, emphasizing the potential for individuals and societies to adopt environmentally friendly practices in the post-pandemic era.

By showcasing these innovative and adaptive responses, this chapter aims to inspire readers and underscore the potential for positive transformations that can arise from adversity. It sets the stage for continued exploration into the societal, economic, and health dimensions of rebuilding and fortifying global systems in the aftermath of this transformative event.

B. Lessons learned and opportunities for growth

In this section of "Unveiling Pain: The Global Impact of COVID-19," we reflect on the profound lessons learned from the challenges of the pandemic and explore the opportunities for growth that have emerged as individuals, communities, and nations navigate the path toward recovery and renewal.

Introduction to Reflection and Renewal

- Defining Lessons Learned: The chapter begins by defining the concept of lessons learned as insights gained from the experiences of the pandemic. It explores how these lessons serve as catalysts for growth, transformation, and renewal.

- Seizing Opportunities for Growth: The narrative underscores the importance of seizing opportunities for growth, emphasizing that resilience and adaptation can pave the way for a future that is both learned and transformed.

Global Solidarity: Unity in Diversity

- The Power of Global Unity: This part delves into the lesson of global solidarity, exploring how the pandemic highlighted the interconnectedness of humanity. It examines instances where nations, organizations, and individuals came together to address shared challenges.

- Building Bridges, Not Walls: The narrative reflects on the importance of building bridges rather than walls, considering how global cooperation can be a powerful force in addressing not only health crises but also broader global issues.

Healthcare Preparedness: Investing in Resilient Systems

- Investing in Healthcare Infrastructure: This section explores the lesson of healthcare preparedness, examining how the pandemic exposed vulnerabilities in healthcare systems. It delves into the importance of investing in resilient healthcare infrastructure, research, and international collaboration.

- Building Resilient Health Systems: The narrative reflects on the need to build resilient health systems capable of responding to crises, emphasizing the lessons learned from the pandemic as a driving force for positive change.

Digital Transformation Acceleration: Embracing the Digital Age

● The Role of Technology in Society: This part highlights the acceleration of digital transformation across various sectors. It explores how the pandemic acted as a catalyst for embracing technology in healthcare, education, work, and daily life.

● Adapting to the Digital Age: The narrative reflects on the adaptability of societies to the digital age, emphasizing the potential for continued innovation and integration of technology into various facets of human existence.

Resilient Economic Models: From Recovery to Sustainability

● Rethinking Economic Systems: This section explores the lesson of rethinking economic models. It examines how the pandemic exposed vulnerabilities in traditional economic structures and fostered discussions about sustainability, equitable growth, and the well-being of individuals.

● Towards Sustainable Economies: The narrative reflects on the potential for transitioning towards more sustainable and inclusive economic models, considering lessons learned about the interconnectedness of economic, social, and environmental well-being.

Education for Adaptability: Nurturing Lifelong Learners

● Adaptability in Education: This part delves into the lesson of adaptability in education. It explores how disruptions in traditional learning models prompted a reevaluation of educational systems, emphasizing the importance of nurturing lifelong learners equipped for continuous adaptation.

● Empowering Students for the Future: The narrative reflects on the need to empower students with skills for the future, considering the evolving landscape of work and the importance of adaptability in the face of uncertainty.

Community Resilience: Strengthening Social Bonds

● The Importance of Community: This section explores the lesson of community resilience, emphasizing how communities that came together during the pandemic demonstrated the strength of social bonds. It examines how shared experiences fostered a sense of belonging and support.

● Building Stronger Communities: The narrative reflects on the importance of building stronger, more resilient communities, considering the lessons learned about the power of mutual aid, compassion, and collaboration.

ENVIRONMENTAL STEWARDSHIP: Sustaining a Healthy Planet

● Lessons from Reduced Human Activity: This part highlights the lessons learned from reduced human activity on the environment. It explores how lockdowns led to temporary improvements in air quality and reduced carbon emissions, offering insights into sustainable living practices.

● Towards Environmental Conservation: The narrative reflects on the potential for incorporating lessons from environmental stewardship into long-term sustainable living practices, considering the interconnectedness of human well-being and planetary health.

Mental Health Prioritization: Breaking the Stigma

● Elevating Mental Health Awareness: This section explores the lesson of prioritizing mental health. It examines how the pandemic brought mental health to the forefront of public discourse, breaking down stigmas and emphasizing the importance of holistic well-being.

● Creating Supportive Societal Structures: The narrative reflects on the need to create supportive societal structures for mental health, considering the lessons learned about resilience, empathy, and the interconnected nature of mental and physical well-being.

Preparedness for Future Challenges: A Call to Action

● Anticipating Future Challenges: This chapter concludes by exploring the lesson of preparedness for future challenges. It examines how the experiences of the pandemic serve as a call to action, urging individuals, communities, and nations to be proactive in addressing and mitigating future crises.

● A Global Commitment to Resilience: The narrative reflects on the potential for a global commitment to resilience, emphasizing the shared responsibility of preparing for and responding to challenges that transcend borders.

By reflecting on these lessons learned and opportunities for growth, this chapter aims to inspire readers to envision a future that is not only better informed but also more resilient, adaptable, and compassionate. It sets the stage for continued exploration into the societal, economic, and health dimensions of rebuilding and fortifying global systems in the aftermath of this transformative event.

1. Reflection on global responses

In this pivotal section of "Unveiling Pain: The Global Impact of COVID-19," we reflect on the diverse and interconnected responses that unfolded across the globe in the face of an unprecedented challenge. This chapter serves as a lens through which we analyze the collective actions, collaborative endeavors, and lessons learned from the global community's response to the COVID-19 pandemic.

Introduction to Global Responses

• Defining Global Solidarity: The chapter begins by defining the concept of global responses as the collaborative efforts of nations, organizations, and individuals to address the multifaceted challenges posed by the pandemic. It explores the interconnectedness of the global community in the face of a shared crisis.

• Navigating a Collective Challenge: The narrative underscores the significance of navigating the pandemic as a collective challenge, emphasizing the role of unity, cooperation, and shared responsibility in shaping global responses.

Early Crisis Management: Lessons from the Initial Response

• Pandemic Preparedness and Initial Responses: This part delves into the early stages of the crisis, exploring lessons learned from pandemic preparedness and the initial responses of nations. It examines the effectiveness of measures such as lockdowns, travel restrictions, and public health campaigns in containing the spread of the virus.

• Adaptability and Learning from Each Other: The narrative reflects on the adaptability of nations and the importance of learning from each other's successes and challenges in the dynamic landscape of a global pandemic.

International Collaboration: Strengths and Limitations

• Collaborative Efforts and Global Initiatives: This section explores international collaboration, examining global initiatives, partnerships, and joint research efforts to develop treatments and vaccines. It assesses the strengths and limitations of collaborative endeavors in addressing the global health crisis.

• Navigating Political and Logistical Challenges: The narrative reflects on the diplomatic, political, and logistical challenges that influenced international collaboration, emphasizing the need for coordinated responses to navigate a crisis that transcends borders.

Inequality in Access to Resources: Gaps in Global Health Equity

● Disparities in Healthcare Access: This part addresses the disparities in access to healthcare resources and vaccines. It explores how global inequities exacerbated the impact of the pandemic on vulnerable populations and discusses efforts to bridge these gaps.

● A Call for Global Health Equity: The narrative reflects on the ethical imperative of addressing healthcare disparities, emphasizing the lessons learned about the interconnectedness of global health and the need for inclusive solutions.

Public Communication and Misinformation: Navigating the Information Landscape

● Communication Strategies: This section examines communication strategies employed by nations and international organizations to disseminate accurate information and combat misinformation. It explores the role of transparency, public engagement, and media literacy in navigating the information landscape.

● Challenges in Information Dissemination: The narrative reflects on the challenges of information dissemination, acknowledging the impact of misinformation on public trust and the importance of fostering a collective sense of responsibility for accurate communication.

National Health Systems: Strengthening and Strain

● Resilience and Strain on Healthcare Systems: This part assesses the resilience and strain experienced by national healthcare systems. It explores lessons learned from the pandemic's impact on healthcare infrastructure, workforce, and the capacity to respond to surges in cases.

• Investment in Healthcare Resilience: The narrative reflects on the imperative of investing in healthcare resilience and preparedness, considering the long-term implications for global health security.

Political Leadership: Challenges and Opportunities

• Leadership Styles and Decision-Making: This section examines different political leadership styles and decision-making processes in responding to the pandemic. It explores how political leaders navigated the complexities of balancing public health with economic and social considerations.

• The Role of Leadership in Crisis: The narrative reflects on the pivotal role of leadership during a crisis, emphasizing the importance of transparency, accountability, and a collaborative approach in addressing global challenges.

Citizen Engagement: Mobilizing Societal Support

• Community Engagement and Compliance: This part explores citizen engagement and the role of societal support in implementing public health measures. It examines how communities mobilized to support healthcare workers, adhere to guidelines, and contribute to the collective effort to curb the spread of the virus.

• Empowering Communities for Resilience: The narrative reflects on the empowerment of communities as active participants in the response to a global crisis, highlighting the lessons learned about the strength of collective action.

Economic Policies: Balancing Health and Economic Priorities

• Policy Responses to Economic Fallout: This section assesses economic policies implemented by nations to mitigate the impact of the pandemic on livelihoods and economies. It explores the balance between health priorities and the need for economic stability.

• Lessons in Economic Resilience: The narrative reflects on the lessons learned about the interconnectedness of health and economic well-being, emphasizing the importance of adaptable economic policies in navigating global challenges.

Reflections on Global Governance and Future Preparedness

• Global Governance Challenges: This chapter concludes by reflecting on global governance challenges and opportunities for future preparedness. It examines the role of international institutions, collaborative frameworks, and the need for a coordinated global response in addressing future pandemics and crises.

• A Call for Collective Responsibility: The narrative reflects on the call for collective responsibility in global governance, emphasizing the imperative of learning from past experiences to fortify international cooperation in the face of future challenges.

By reflecting on global responses to the COVID-19 pandemic, this chapter aims to provide insights into the complexities, achievements, and areas for improvement in addressing global health crises. It sets the stage for continued exploration into the societal, economic, and health dimensions of rebuilding and fortifying global systems in the aftermath of this transformative event.

2. Building a more resilient future

In this transformative segment of "Unveiling Pain: The Global Impact of COVID-19," we delve into the strategies and considerations for building a more resilient future in the wake of the pandemic. This chapter serves as a roadmap for individuals, communities, and nations to learn from the challenges faced and collectively contribute to shaping a more adaptable and fortified world.

Introduction to Resilience Building

• Defining Resilience in the Post-Pandemic Era: The chapter begins by defining resilience as the capacity to withstand, adapt to, and recover from challenges. It explores how the experiences of the pandemic lay the groundwork for intentional efforts to build resilience in various facets of society.

• A Call to Action: The narrative underscores the call to action for individuals, communities, and policymakers to actively contribute to the collective endeavor of building a more resilient future.

Global Health Security: Strengthening Preparedness and Collaboration

• Investing in Global Health Infrastructure: This part explores the imperative of investing in global health infrastructure. It examines how nations can collaborate to strengthen early detection systems, research capabilities, and the equitable distribution of healthcare resources.

• International Collaboration for Health Resilience: The narrative reflects on the lessons learned about the interconnectedness of global health and emphasizes the need for sustained international collaboration to enhance health security.

Technological Innovation and Preparedness: Harnessing the Power of Technology

• Advancements in Healthcare Technology: This section delves into the role of technological innovation in healthcare. It explores how emerging technologies such as telemedicine, artificial intelligence, and data analytics can be harnessed to enhance healthcare delivery, early detection, and response mechanisms.

• Adapting to the Digital Age: The narrative reflects on the transformative potential of technology in shaping a healthcare landscape that is adaptive, efficient, and resilient.

Economic Resilience: Balancing Stability and Innovation

● Diversification and Adaptive Economic Models: This part addresses the need for economic resilience. It explores how nations can diversify their economies, promote innovation, and implement adaptive economic models that balance stability with the capacity to withstand unforeseen challenges.

● Sustainable Development Goals as a Framework: The narrative reflects on the Sustainable Development Goals as a framework for building economically resilient and socially inclusive societies.

Education for the Future: Fostering Lifelong Learning and Adaptability

● Adaptive Learning Environments: This section focuses on transforming education for adaptability. It explores the integration of digital learning platforms, the development of skills for the future, and the creation of adaptive learning environments that prepare individuals for a rapidly evolving world.

● Empowering Lifelong Learners: The narrative reflects on the role of education in empowering individuals as lifelong learners, capable of navigating the uncertainties of the future.

Community and Social Resilience: Strengthening Social Bonds

● Community-Led Initiatives: This part explores the role of community-led initiatives in fostering social resilience. It examines how communities can strengthen social bonds, address inequalities, and provide support systems that enhance overall resilience.

● Inclusivity and Empowerment: The narrative reflects on the importance of inclusivity and empowerment within communities, emphasizing the role of social cohesion in building resilience.

Environmental Sustainability: Prioritizing Planet Health

- Sustainable Practices and Policies: This section addresses the intersection of environmental and societal resilience. It explores how sustainable practices, policies, and global cooperation can contribute to a healthier planet and more resilient communities.

- The Role of Green Technologies: The narrative reflects on the role of green technologies and eco-friendly initiatives in promoting environmental sustainability for long-term resilience.

Mental Health and Well-being: Integrating Mental Health into Public Health:

- Mental Health Awareness and Support Systems: This part focuses on the integration of mental health into public health priorities. It explores the importance of mental health awareness, destigmatization, and the establishment of robust support systems for individuals and communities.

- Holistic Approaches to Well-being: The narrative reflects on the need for holistic approaches to well-being, recognizing mental health as an integral component of overall resilience.

Governance for Crisis Management: Adaptive Policies and Inclusive Decision-Making

- Adaptive Governance Structures: This section delves into the need for adaptive governance structures. It explores how governments can implement inclusive decision-making processes, flexible policies, and proactive strategies for crisis management.

- Transparency and Accountability: The narrative reflects on the principles of transparency, accountability, and adaptability as foundational elements of effective governance for resilience.

Crisis Preparedness and Response: Learning from Adversity

● Building Institutional Capacities: This chapter concludes by emphasizing the importance of crisis preparedness and response. It explores how institutions can build capacities for anticipating, responding to, and recovering from future crises.

● A Resilient Global Community: The narrative reflects on the lessons learned from adversity, emphasizing the potential for a resilient global community that is better equipped to navigate the uncertainties of tomorrow.

By outlining these strategies for building a more resilient future, this chapter aims to inspire readers to actively engage in the collective effort to shape a world that is adaptive, inclusive, and capable of withstanding the challenges that may lie ahead. It sets the stage for continued exploration into the societal, economic, and health dimensions of rebuilding and fortifying global systems in the aftermath of this transformative event.

Conclusion

As we draw the final pages of "Unveiling Pain: The Global Impact of COVID-19," the narrative unveils not just a chronicle of suffering but a testament to the indomitable human spirit, collective resilience, and the potential for transformative change in the face of adversity.

A Tapestry of Global Struggle

- The pages of this book have woven a tapestry of global struggle, where the threads of individual pain converge into a shared narrative of loss, resilience, and perseverance. The pandemic, with its far-reaching tendrils, has touched every corner of the world, leaving no nation untouched.

Lessons from Pain

- In the wake of immense pain, we find the silver linings of lessons learned. The collective responses, both remarkable and flawed, have illuminated the strengths and vulnerabilities of societies. From healthcare systems strained to the brink to economic structures tested beyond their limits, each challenge is an opportunity for growth and improvement.

The Human Toll: A Symphony of Loss and Grit

- The chapters unfolded a symphony of loss, where mortality rates soared, lives were irrevocably altered, and the healthcare systems strained under the weight of the pandemic's relentless assault. Yet, amidst this somber melody, stories of personal grit and resilience emerged, demonstrating the tenacity of the human spirit.

Economic Fallout: Navigating Uncharted Waters

- The economic fallout cast a long shadow, with global recessions, business closures, and the specter of unemployment haunting the world. As we explored these challenges, we also witnessed the emergence of innovation, adaptability, and a renewed focus on sustainable economic models.

Educational Disruption: A Fork in the Learning Path

- The disruption to education reshaped the landscape of learning, laying bare the digital divide and inequities in educational access. However, within this disruption, we found the seeds of future possibilities — a potential shift towards more inclusive, adaptable, and technology-enhanced education.

Mental Health Struggles: Breaking the Silence

- The toll on mental health became a poignant theme, where isolation and uncertainty gave rise to a surge in mental health disorders. Yet, within the struggles, there emerged a growing acknowledgment of the importance of mental well-being and a collective effort to break the silence surrounding mental health issues.

Strain on Healthcare Systems: A Battle on the Frontlines

- The strain on healthcare systems took center stage, with overwhelmed hospitals, exhausted healthcare workers, and resource allocation challenges. Amidst the chaos, stories from the frontline highlighted the dedication, sacrifice, and resilience of those who stood as the vanguard against the invisible enemy.

Social and Cultural Disruption: A Shift in Norms

- Social and cultural disruptions unfolded as societal norms shifted, impacting social interactions and cultural practices. The narratives explored the nuances of change, revealing both the challenges and the potential for a reimagined, more inclusive societal framework.

Hope and Resilience: Acts of Kindness and Innovations

• The exploration of hope and resilience uncovered tales of extraordinary kindness, solidarity, and innovation. From community support initiatives to technological adaptations, these stories illuminated the strength embedded within communities and the human capacity to innovate even in the darkest of times.

Building a Resilient Future: Lessons and Opportunities

• The final chapters outlined a roadmap for building a more resilient future. Drawing lessons from the pain of the pandemic, we explored avenues for global health security, technological innovation, economic resilience, education reform, and the imperative of prioritizing mental health.

A Call to Action

• As the final chapter unfolds, it extends a resounding call to action. It invites individuals, communities, and nations to actively engage in the collective effort to shape a world that is not just rebuilt but fortified against future challenges. The lessons learned, the innovations witnessed, and the global responses examined serve as guideposts for a future characterized by adaptability, inclusivity, and collective responsibility.

In the Wake of Transformation

• The concluding pages reflect not only on the pain endured but also on the transformations that emerged. It is a narrative that looks forward with hope, acknowledging the scars left by the pandemic while recognizing the potential for renewal, growth, and a future forged in the crucible of shared global experiences.

In closing, "Unveiling Pain: The Global Impact of COVID-19" is not just a chronicle of a pandemic; it is a testament to the resilience of the human spirit and the boundless potential for positive change in the wake of crisis. As we turn the last page, may it serve as a catalyst for reflection, understanding, and a collective commitment to building a world that is not only restored but strengthened by the challenges it has faced.

A. Recap of the global pain caused by COVID-19

In revisiting the global pain caused by COVID-19, let us reflect on the profound impact that this unprecedented pandemic has had on individuals, communities, and nations across the world.

High Mortality Rates and Loss of Lives

- The pandemic unfolded as a relentless force, bringing with it high mortality rates and the profound loss of lives. From bustling metropolises to remote villages, the virus spared no corner of the globe, leaving behind a trail of grief, mourning, and empty spaces once filled with the warmth of loved ones.

- Statistics on Global Death Toll: The staggering statistics on the global death toll painted a grim picture of the scale of human tragedy, revealing not just numbers but the stories, dreams, and potential extinguished by the invisible foe.

- Personal Stories and Anecdotes: Intertwined with the statistics were personal stories and anecdotes, each a testament to the individual lives lost and the ripple effects of grief reverberating through families and communities.

Long-Term Health Effects

- Beyond the immediate threat to life, the pandemic ushered in a wave of long-term health effects. Lingering symptoms, often referred to as "long COVID," became a pervasive challenge, affecting survivors with a spectrum of physical and neurological issues.

• Overview of Lingering Health Issues: This segment provided an overview of the lingering health issues faced by survivors, ranging from respiratory complications to neurological symptoms, illustrating the complexity and variability of the post-COVID health landscape.

• Impact on Individuals and Healthcare Systems: The discussion extended to the impact on individuals grappling with ongoing health challenges and the strain imposed on healthcare systems tasked with addressing the multifaceted needs of long-term COVID patients.

Economic Fallout: Global Recession and Economic Downturn

• The economic fallout emerged as a parallel crisis, with a global recession and economic downturn reshaping financial landscapes. Businesses shuttered, employment rates plummeted, and the economic hardships unleashed by the pandemic cast a long shadow over livelihoods worldwide.

• Effects on Employment and Income: This section delved into the effects on employment and income, examining the widespread job losses, furloughs, and financial uncertainties faced by individuals and families.

• Business Closures and Bankruptcies: The narrative explored the widespread closures of businesses, both small and large, and the haunting specter of bankruptcies that reverberated through industries, leaving economic scars that would take years to heal.

Educational Disruption: Closure of Schools and Universities

• Educational institutions faced unprecedented disruptions, with schools and universities closing their physical doors in the wake of the pandemic. The abrupt shift to remote learning laid bare the digital divide and underscored the challenges of ensuring continued access to education.

● Impact on Students and Educators: This segment delved into the impact on students and educators, exploring the struggles of adapting to virtual learning environments, the disparities in educational access, and the broader implications for the future of education.

● Digital Divide and Unequal Access to Education: The narrative highlighted the digital divide as a central issue, emphasizing the unequal access to education and the imperative of addressing these disparities for a more inclusive learning landscape.

Future Implications for the Global Workforce

● The closure of schools and economic disruptions had profound implications for the global workforce. The traditional notions of work and education underwent seismic shifts, prompting a reevaluation of skills, career paths, and the future landscape of employment.

● Changes in Skill Requirements: This section explored the changes in skill requirements driven by the evolving demands of the post-pandemic workforce. The narrative delved into the skills deemed essential for navigating the uncertainties of the future job market.

● Shifting Dynamics of Education and Work: The discussion extended to the shifting dynamics of education and work, highlighting the interconnectedness of learning and employment and the need for a more fluid and adaptable approach to career development.

Mental Health Struggles: Isolation and Social Distancing

• The isolation imposed by social distancing measures became a silent pandemic within the pandemic, giving rise to profound mental health struggles. The challenges of coping with uncertainty, loneliness, and the psychological toll of the crisis became increasingly evident.

• Impact on Mental Well-being: This segment explored the impact on mental well-being, delving into the emotional strain experienced by individuals isolated from social support systems and grappling with the pervasive anxiety and stress induced by the pandemic.

• Rise in Mental Health Disorders: The narrative highlighted the alarming rise in mental health disorders, emphasizing the need for increased awareness, destigmatization, and robust support systems to address the mental health challenges precipitated by the pandemic.

Strain on Healthcare Systems: Overwhelmed Hospitals and Healthcare Workers

• The strain on healthcare systems emerged as a central theme, with overwhelmed hospitals and healthcare workers facing unprecedented challenges. The narratives from the frontlines provided a glimpse into the heroic efforts, sacrifices, and resilience of those battling the pandemic at the forefront.

• Stories from Frontline Workers: This section presented stories from frontline workers, offering firsthand accounts of the physical and emotional toll experienced by healthcare professionals. It underscored the extraordinary dedication and sacrifices made in the pursuit of saving lives.

• Struggles with Resource Allocation: The narrative delved into the struggles with resource allocation, exploring the ethical dilemmas and difficult decisions faced by healthcare professionals as they navigated the scarcity of medical supplies, ventilators, and critical care resources.

Global Vaccine Distribution Challenges: Disparities in Vaccine Access

● The development and distribution of vaccines became a beacon of hope in the fight against the pandemic. However, the challenges of ensuring equitable access to vaccines highlighted global disparities, with certain nations and populations facing barriers to vaccination.

● Disparities in Vaccine Access: This segment addressed the disparities in vaccine access, examining the hurdles faced by low-income countries and marginalized communities in securing sufficient vaccine doses. It underscored the urgency of addressing these disparities for a truly effective global response.

● Implications for Global Health Security: The narrative expanded on the implications for global health security, emphasizing that a comprehensive and equitable approach to vaccine distribution is integral to achieving widespread immunity and preventing the resurgence of the virus.

Social and Cultural Disruption: Changes in Societal Norms and Behaviors

● Social and cultural norms underwent profound changes, reshaping how societies interacted, celebrated, and mourned. The disruptions to daily life revealed both the fragility and adaptability of cultural practices in the face of a global crisis.

● Impact on Social Interactions: This section explored the impact on social interactions, from physical distancing measures to the rise of virtual communication. It highlighted the challenges faced by communities in maintaining social bonds while adhering to public health guidelines.

B. Call to action for a united and collaborative response

In the wake of the global pain inflicted by COVID-19, the imperative for a united and collaborative response emerges as a guiding principle for charting a path towards recovery and resilience. The chapters of suffering and the lessons learned serve as a clarion call for collective action, urging individuals, communities, and nations to unite in the face of shared challenges.

Recognizing Interconnectedness

- The first step in the call to action is a recognition of the interconnectedness that binds the global community. The pandemic has laid bare the fact that the health and well-being of one nation are inseparable from that of another. In acknowledging this interdependence, we pave the way for a more empathetic and collaborative world.

Global Health Solidarity: Strengthening International Cooperation

- A united response in the realm of global health is paramount. Strengthening international cooperation and fostering global health solidarity are essential components of this call to action. This involves equitable access to vaccines, sharing of medical knowledge, and collaborative efforts to fortify healthcare systems worldwide.

Information Sharing and Combating Misinformation

- In the digital age, information flows rapidly, influencing public perception and shaping responses. A call to action involves a commitment to responsible information sharing, transparent communication, and the collective effort to combat misinformation. By fostering a global environment of accurate knowledge, communities can make informed decisions and better respond to crises.

Economic Collaboration and Inclusive Recovery

• The economic fallout from the pandemic underscores the need for collaborative economic policies. A call to action in the economic sphere involves nations working together to ensure inclusive recovery, support vulnerable populations, and implement policies that balance the restoration of economic stability with considerations for social well-being.

Education for All: Bridging the Digital Divide:

• As education faced disruption, the call to action in this realm involves bridging the digital divide and ensuring that education is accessible to all. Collaborative efforts between governments, educational institutions, and the private sector can lead to innovative solutions that empower students and educators, regardless of their socio-economic background.

Mental Health Advocacy: Breaking the Stigma Globally

• Mental health struggles, exacerbated by the pandemic, necessitate a global call to action for mental health advocacy. Breaking the stigma surrounding mental health requires concerted efforts to raise awareness, provide support systems, and foster a global culture that prioritizes mental well-being as an integral part of public health.

Supporting Healthcare Systems: Global Solidarity for Resilient Systems

• Healthcare systems strained by the pandemic need sustained support. A call to action involves global solidarity to strengthen healthcare infrastructure, invest in medical research, and ensure that frontline workers receive the resources and recognition they deserve. This collaborative effort is essential for building resilient healthcare systems prepared for future challenges.

Equitable Vaccine Distribution: A Moral Imperative

● Ensuring equitable access to vaccines is not just a health imperative but a moral one. The call to action involves nations, pharmaceutical companies, and international organizations working together to overcome barriers to vaccine distribution. Only through collective efforts can we achieve widespread immunity and bring an end to the pandemic.

Cultural Understanding and Inclusivity: Embracing Diversity

● Social and cultural disruptions call for a call to action centered around cultural understanding and inclusivity. Embracing diversity and recognizing the richness of different cultural practices contribute to a more resilient global society. Communities should strive for inclusivity, learn from one another, and celebrate the strength found in diversity.

Environmental Collaboration: Nurturing the Planet

● The environmental challenges highlighted by the pandemic demand a collaborative response for the health of the planet. A call to action involves nations working together to adopt sustainable practices, reduce carbon emissions, and prioritize environmental conservation. By recognizing the shared responsibility for the health of the Earth, we contribute to a more resilient and sustainable future.

Building a Future of Hope: Learning and Adapting

● The call to action is an invitation to build a future characterized by hope, learning, and adaptation. It is a commitment to learning from the painful lessons of the pandemic, adapting to the evolving global landscape, and fostering a collective resilience that can withstand the challenges of an uncertain future.

Fostering Innovation and Research: A Shared Endeavor

• Innovation and research are vital components of the call to action. A collaborative approach to scientific endeavors, technological advancements, and medical research can lead to breakthroughs that benefit humanity globally. By fostering an environment of shared knowledge and innovation, we contribute to a more resilient and prepared world.

In the face of unprecedented challenges, the call to action resonates as a beacon of hope. It is a collective endeavor that transcends borders, ideologies, and differences, recognizing our shared humanity. As individuals and nations respond to this call, we embark on a journey toward a future characterized not only by recovery but by a newfound strength forged in unity and collaboration. Together, we can build a world that is not just restored but resilient, adaptive, and ready to face whatever challenges lie ahead.

C. Optimism for the post-pandemic era

In the aftermath of the global pain inflicted by COVID-19, a spirit of optimism emerges, illuminating the path toward a post-pandemic era marked by hope, renewal, and the potential for positive transformation. This chapter celebrates the resilience of the human spirit and envisions a future shaped by collective efforts to rebuild, learn, and grow.

Healing and Restoration

• The post-pandemic era brings with it a collective desire for healing and restoration. Communities, individuals, and nations unite in the shared aspiration to rebuild what was lost, mend the wounds inflicted by the pandemic, and embark on a journey toward renewed well-being.

Scientific Advancements and Medical Breakthroughs

• Optimism is fueled by the remarkable scientific advancements and medical breakthroughs achieved during the pandemic. The development and distribution of vaccines stand as a testament to human ingenuity and the potential for collaborative efforts to overcome even the most formidable challenges.

Global Solidarity: Strengthening Bonds Across Borders

• The shared experience of the pandemic fosters a sense of global solidarity. Optimism for the post-pandemic era is grounded in the recognition that, despite borders and differences, humanity is interconnected. Nations collaborate, share resources, and work together to address not only the aftermath of the pandemic but also future global challenges.

Resilient Healthcare Systems: Learning and Strengthening

• The strain on healthcare systems during the pandemic becomes a catalyst for positive change. Optimism arises from the commitment to learn from the challenges faced, strengthen healthcare infrastructure, and invest in the well-being of healthcare workers. The result is the emergence of more resilient and adaptable healthcare systems.

Education Transformation: Embracing Innovation

• The disruptions to education prompt a wave of innovation and transformation. Optimism is rooted in the belief that the post-pandemic era will witness a reimagining of education, where technology is harnessed for inclusive learning, and institutions adapt to foster resilience and lifelong learning.

Economic Recovery and Sustainable Practices

• Optimism for economic recovery is coupled with a commitment to sustainable practices. Nations seize the opportunity to rebuild economies with a focus on resilience, inclusivity, and environmental sustainability. The post-pandemic era becomes a canvas for innovative economic models that prioritize both prosperity and planetary health.

Mental Health Prioritization: Destigmatizing and Supporting

- The struggles with mental health during the pandemic inspire a collective commitment to prioritize mental well-being. Optimism is grounded in efforts to destigmatize mental health issues, provide robust support systems, and integrate mental health into broader public health initiatives.

Innovative Technologies: Shaping a Digital Future

- The acceleration of digital transformation during the pandemic opens doors to an era of innovative technologies. Optimism is fueled by the potential of these technologies to shape a more connected, efficient, and technologically advanced world, fostering progress in healthcare, education, and various sectors.

CULTURAL RENAISSANCE: Celebrating Diversity and Inclusivity

- The disruptions to societal norms lead to a cultural renaissance marked by a celebration of diversity and inclusivity. Optimism arises from the recognition that the post-pandemic era is an opportunity to build societies that embrace differences, promote equality, and foster a sense of belonging for all.

Environmental Consciousness: A Greener Future

- The environmental disruptions during the pandemic prompt a renewed focus on environmental consciousness. Optimism is grounded in the commitment to build a greener future, where nations collaborate to address climate change, protect biodiversity, and prioritize sustainable practices for the well-being of the planet.

Community Empowerment: Building Stronger Bonds

- The challenges faced by communities during the pandemic inspire a sense of empowerment. Optimism stems from the understanding that communities have the capacity to build stronger bonds, support one another, and collectively navigate challenges, fostering a sense of resilience and solidarity.

Hopeful Narratives and Acts of Kindness: Inspiring Positive Change

- Optimism is woven into the fabric of hopeful narratives and acts of kindness that emerged during the pandemic. These stories inspire positive change, highlighting the inherent goodness within humanity and the capacity for individuals to make a meaningful difference in the lives of others.

In the post-pandemic era, optimism becomes a driving force for positive change. It is a collective mindset that propels individuals and nations toward a future marked by resilience, compassion, and a shared commitment to building a world that is not only restored but transformed for the better. As we step into this new era, the pages turn with hope, inviting us to contribute to the narrative of renewal and embrace the possibilities that lie ahead.

Also by Swatantra Bahadur

Breaking Barriers: LGBTQ Rights and Social Justice
Blossom with confidence
"Depression: A Roller Coaster Ride"
Finding Your Voice
Rahul Gandhi: The Untold Story
100 Aspects on Nature
Love By An Introvert
Man Of Golden India "Narendra Modi"
India " Unity lies in Diversity"
Indian's Heritage of Kashi "Varanasi"
"The Power of Voice: Lawyer in a Black Coat"
Shri Ram Janmabhumi "Ayodhya"
Social Media and Youth: Navigating the Digital Landscape
Jai Shri Hanuman Garhi "Ayodhya"
"Unveiling Pain: The Global Impact of COVID-19"

About the Author

Instagram Id - swatantrabahadur15